Contents

Sarum Chronicle is published on behalf of its editorial team by Hobnob Press, P O Box 1838, East Knoyle, Salisbury SP3 6FA, to whom all orders, correspondence and contributions for future issues should be addressed. Potential contributors are invited to apply for a style sheet.

Front cover illustration: The 'Busy Bees' preparing for inspection. The 5th Salisbury Girl Guide Company on their summer camp in Wilton Park, c. 1924 (WSA 2777/360/1, by kind permission of the Wiltshire & Swindon History Centre, see page 24)

Sarum Chronicle – The Future

With this issue *Sarum Chronicle* celebrates the end of its first decade. It seems only a short time ago that the original editorial board (John Elliott joined us later, in 2003) sat round a table debating the merits of possible names such as *Salisbury Examiner*, *Observer* or *Oracle* before settling on our present title. During those 10 years there have been over 50 major articles and about a dozen shorter contributions and book reviews. Though we have not managed to cover as much of our self-designated area of the city and a 10 mile radius as we would have liked, we have had articles about Amesbury, Bemerton, Dinton, Laverstock, Tisbury, Wardour and Wilton. Our subjects have ranged from academies to women's suffrage via archaeology and architecture, cemeteries, chapels, churches and the Cathedral, disease and disaster, eccentric sculptors and eminent citizens, farming and fallen women, maps, museums and music, policing and prisons, theatres and the Battle of Trafalgar to name just a few. An index to the first 5 volumes appears in issue 5, 2005.

We would like to take this opportunity to thank all our contributors and other supporters, in particular the Hatcher Review Trust whose financial assistance made the launch of this journal possible. However, the grant that they gave us has now been used up and so in order to continue there have to be some changes. From issue 11 onwards *Sarum Chronicle* will be produced and distributed by the Sarum Chronicle Group who will also oversee any future books in the *Sarum Studies* series. The price (unchanged for 10 years) will have to rise, though we hope that future issues will contain more pages and colour illustrations. To achieve a sustainable future we need to expand our existing group of subscribers – who will get future issues at a reduced price. So please fill out the enclosed form, encourage your friends to buy a copy – and tell us of any outlet that would be happy to sell issues for us. Correspondence, by post or email, and proposals for articles, should continue to be directed to Hobnob Press (PO Box 1838, East Knoyle, Salisbury SP3 6FA), from whom a stylesheet for contributors and copies of previous issues may be obtained.

Looking forward to the next 10 years

John Chandler, John Elliott, Jane Howells,
Sue Johnson, Ruth Newman, Margaret Smith

Dr Roberts's Clock Tower

Keith Blake

Gifts can sometimes have consequences unforeseen by donors. When Dr Roberts decided to present Salisbury with a clock in memory of his wife Arabella, who died on 23 January 1892,[1] he could hardly have imagined the controversy that his offer would provoke.

John Roberts was a native of North Wales. He was educated at Trinity College Dublin and Edinburgh University, where he qualified as doctor of medicine in 1845, and came to Salisbury in 1854 to practise at the Infirmary. In 1874 he was appointed honorary consulting physician, a post he was to hold until the end of his life, while at the same time building up an extensive private practice in the city. It was said that 'he devoted a great deal of time and energy to the poor, setting apart certain hours of the day for the giving of free advice'.[2]

In February 1892 the Town Clerk reported to Salisbury Town Council that Dr Roberts had written suggesting that 'an illuminated clock would be both useful and ornamental in Salisbury' and offering to pay for both a turret and clock mechanism.[3] The Council instructed the City Lands Committee to investigate suitable sites, and the Council's surveyor was to submit sketches of suitable towers. To assess the visibility of the proposed clock, poles were to be put up in the Market Square, at Fisherton Bridge, and at the junction of the Canal, Catherine, Milford and Queen Streets. The surveyor was also instructed 'to erect for the period of one week a wooden octagonal base of a size he would advise' at each of the sites to determine their suitability.[4]

All this activity did not go unnoticed. On 12 March 'a citizen' wrote to the *Salisbury and Winchester Journal*:

> The most suitable site on which to erect this generous gift of Dr Roberts appears to be the local question of the hour. Of all the places where I hear trial of effect is being made by the erection of scaffold poles, one in particular should commend itself to our notice as being highly suitable, and where it is to be hoped the authorities will decide on placing it, namely, the east corner lawn front of the Salisbury Infirmary.
>
> The large open space around would give a bold relief to the tower, and it would be to the bridge a miniature Big Ben of Westminster, a beacon timekeeper to the

citizens and visitors. Considering the many years' professional services so kindly and beneficially rendered to the Infirmary by Dr Roberts and his attachment to it, this site of all others would probably be the most acceptable to him.'

The *Journal* reported on 26 March that the City Lands Committee, having met three times, had presented its findings to the Town Council. Apart from considering a freestanding tower, the Committee had also looked at the possibility of incorporating the clock in an existing building. One such proposal involving St Thomas' tower had caused misgivings among the clergy and the other – the roof of the Council House – had 'architectural disadvantages'. The Committee recommended a tower on a site near the Infirmary on the grounds that a clock there would meet Dr Roberts' criteria by being both useful and ornamental.

This did not meet with immediate agreement. The main objection was that fewer people would see the clock at the Infirmary site than at a more central location such as the Market Square and so the usefulness criterion would only be partly fulfilled. Popular opinion seemed to favour a central site. At this point the results of the experiments were revealed: the octagon base had been in place at the Catherine Street junction 'for a day and a half, which was quite long enough to prove that that site was altogether unsuitable for the purpose'. As for the Market Square, its beauty lay in its openness and if councillors required an instance of how a beautiful open space could be spoiled they should consider what had recently happened to Plymouth Hoe, which was now cluttered with statues. The possibility of a turret on the Council House roof was examined, bearing in mind what had been achieved at Portsmouth Town Hall; there was however doubt as to whether the building would support the weight of a clock, and besides here only one face would be seen whereas in an open space such as the Infirmary site all four faces would be visible. A clock at the Infirmary would also be useful to people en route to the railway station, though it was suggested that anyone relying on a clock so far from the station would probably miss their train. In any case, people in the Market Square could hear (even if they could not always see) the existing clock on St Thomas' tower.

What seems to have clinched the matter was that Dr Roberts had been consulted and had 'expressed himself highly pleased that there was a prospect of the clock and tower being erected on that [ie the Infirmary] site'. But opinions remained divided and it was only by the slenderest of majorities (one vote) that the Council eventually resolved to ask the Infirmary to make available, by sale to Dr Roberts, a piece of land large enough for a tower carrying a four sided non-striking clock.

By October the Infirmary committee had agreed to sell 20 square feet of land as a site for the tower for the nominal sum of £5.[5] A design competition had been held (first prize £60) and a contract had been let for the building of the tower at a cost of £400. In November the Council accepted the tender of Messrs John Smith and Sons of Derby for the clock. The tendered price was £78. There was a suggestion that the work be given to a local firm, but tenders from local clock manufacturers had all been higher.[6]

In October it had been forecast that the tower would be completed by January 1893.[7] Not for the last time such an estimate proved to be too optimistic, and on 6 May 1893 the *Journal* reported that complaints had been made about delays in the building work. There were rumours that money had run out and it had become 'a laughing stock'. In June the Town Clerk reported that the clock 'is being tested, and will be set in motion 3 weeks hence'.[8] Dr Roberts had been consulted and (provided that a plaque was incorporated commemorating his wife) did not want a handing over ceremony to take place, and so (it seems) completion of the tower was unremarked.

The firm that installed the clock mechanism (Smith of Derby) was still responsible for maintenance when, in December 1970, it replaced the original gravity mechanism with a more modern movement at a cost of £210.[9] Smith's sold the original clock mechanism to a customer in Providence, USA.[10] In 1997, the new mechanism was completely refurbished and updated to include automatic adjustment for British Summer Time. At the same time the tower itself

The clock tower under repair, June 1957. A photograph taken by the late Austin Underwood, from the collection of Peter Daniels. All rights reserved.

was restored, the main contractors for this work being R Moulding and Co of South Newton, with Keystone as specialist sub contractors. Chilmark stone was used, from the quarry that had provided the original.[11] Smith of Derby continues to be responsible for maintaining the clock, and so this firm has now been providing a service to the City for over 100 years.

Dr Robert's clock tower is now a well-known landmark, and has been appearing on postcards since 1910.[12] The arguments over its siting are long forgotten. Doubtless the good doctor would be happy that, even in an age when almost everyone has a watch the accuracy of which would have astonished the Victorians, his generous gift is still proving 'useful and ornamental' to his adopted city.

The now rather worn inscription. © 2010 Sue Johnson

Notes

1   Death notice in the *Salisbury and Winchester Journal* (SJL) 30 January 1892
2   From Dr Roberts' obituary, SJ 3 November 1906
3   SJL 6 February 1892
4   SJL 26 March 1892
5   *A history of Salisbury Infirmary* – Charles Haskins, 1922, p26
6   SJL 12 November 1892, and sales ledger entry supplied by Smith of Derby
7   SJL 8 October 1892
8   SJL 3 June 1893
9   Copy invoice supplied by Smith of Derby
10 Information supplied by Smith of Derby
11 *The Bulletin* issue 55 - Salisbury District Council 4 July 1997 (via the Wiltshire ephemera collection, Salisbury Library local studies collection FIS004)
12 For an example, see p67 in *Salisbury in old picture postcards*, Alan A Richardson, Zambottel/Netherlands 1983.

Special thanks to P Daniels of Active UK (Visual Communications) Ltd for finding time in a busy schedule to provide the illustration.

The Rise and Decline of Quakerism in South Wiltshire[1]

Kay S Taylor with a contribution by Sue Johnson

> In apparel they are modest, in meats and drinks temperate; that they may have wherewith to give a portion to the afflicted . . . The customs of the world which are foolish and vain, wherein there is no true service to God nor man, they cannot countenance . . . They are willing to give up all that they may follow the leadings of the Life of Christ Jesus their Lord . . . And they do all these things in the integrity and simplicity of their hearts towards God, not thinking thereby to merit life or engage His love and favour by what they can do'. (John Whitehead 1661)[2]

Introduction

Members of the Religious Society of Friends, also known as Friends or Quakers, believe that all people are equal under God and that each person has an individual relationship with God. They first emerged as a recognisable entity in England in the middle of the seventeenth century, as like-minded seekers of religious truth, calling themselves the Children of Light. These 'seekers' developed a loose association of meetings during the upheavals of the English Civil Wars, consolidating into a religious sect during the Interregnum (1649-1660). Quaker missionaries, initially from the north of England and then sent out by leading Friends in London, had arrived in North Wiltshire in the early 1650s to proclaim the Quaker message, which gradually spread throughout the county. From the start their unconventional behaviour marked them out for official opprobrium. Hostile pamphlets depicted Quakers as 'a dangerous sort of people', with many clergymen keen to foster popular suspicions that Quakers were plotting sedition at their meetings.[3] After the Restoration, the government regarded all religious dissidents, including Quakers and Catholics, as subversive and potentially revolutionary groups that needed to be suppressed. They were targeted through a series of laws, known collectively as the Clarendon Code, which imposed severe penalties for a range of offences linked to worshipping outside the Established Church. Quaker meetings were settled in the Salisbury area later than in the north of the county, probably due to Salisbury's standing a major ecclesiastical centre.

Seth Ward, who was appointed as Bishop of Salisbury in 1667, was renowned for his stand against religious nonconformity and remained in post until his death in 1689 – the year that the Act of Toleration was passed.[4]

South Wiltshire Quakers and the Friends' network of meetings

Soon after Wiltshire Friends started meeting together for worship they began to develop a network of meetings to support and regulate their members. The majority of these meetings were situated in the north and west of the county - the area most easily accessed by missionaries travelling along the Great West Road from London to Bristol. Particular Meetings, where men and women Friends gathered together for worship, served a number of local parishes and were usually known by the name of one of those parishes. Regional Monthly Meetings to deal with Quakers' business affairs were attended by male representatives from each area's Particular Meetings. Similarly representatives from the Monthly Meetings attended a Quarterly Meeting for the whole county. Monthly Meeting minute books for Friends in the north-west and north-east of the county have survived from 1669 and 1677 respectively,[5] while the earliest surviving Wiltshire Quarterly Meeting minutes date from 1678.[6] The Lavington Monthly Meeting became the focus for Friends from across the whole of central and south Wiltshire but its earliest surviving minute book only dates from 1692.[7] Lavington seems to have been chosen for the Friends' third divisional Monthly Meeting because its position on the edge of Salisbury Plain meant that it was more conveniently situated for many southern Friends than the town of Devizes. It also had the advantage of being home to the prominent Quaker families of the Selfes and the Gyes.

During the 1660s and 1670s the Wiltshire Friends' network of meetings was formalised and integrated into that of the national Quaker movement, which held a Yearly Meeting in London for representatives from across the country. The structure of the national movement was not intended to be hierarchical but provided a convenient way of passing information between Friends in London and the provinces.

Although representatives from all the south Wiltshire meetings were technically affiliated to the Lavington Monthly Meeting, Friends in the Salisbury area had always been something of an anomaly. The vast expanse of Salisbury Plain proved to be a physical barrier between the Quakers from the Salisbury area and the rest of the county, and Friends in Alderbury and Fovant often preferred to send their own independent representatives to the Quarterly Meeting. After the establishment of the Stapleford Particular Meeting in 1686, the Wiltshire clerk often erroneously classified Alderbury and Fovant as one meeting. Eventually the Alderbury Particular Meeting was replaced by one in Salisbury itself. The establishment of the short-lived Salisbury Monthly Meeting in 1704[8] will be discussed below.

Chart 1: The Structure of the Wiltshire Friends' Meeting Network

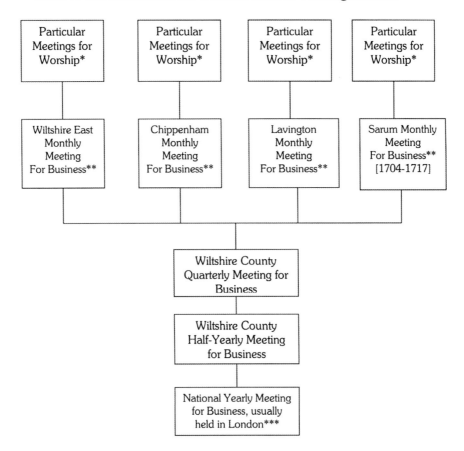

* Particular meetings were joint meetings for worship, but sent male representatives to the monthly meeting, where the Society's business was discussed. Each meeting attracted Friends from a number of neighbouring parishes. Representatives from the monthly meetings represented each district at the county's quarterly meeting, and representatives from that meeting represented the county at the yearly national meeting.
**From the late 1670s women held their own monthly business meetings in parallel with the men's monthly meetings, and by 1696 they also had their own half-yearly meeting, in parallel with the men's meeting.
***This structure was not intended to imply a chain of command down from London, but was a practical measure to enable representatives from all the men's meetings to take part in the wider decision making of the Society.

The earliest references to south Wiltshire Quakers occur in the Dorset Friends' registers of births, burials, and marriage for the 1660s, rather than in the Wiltshire annals.[9] We know from these Dorset records that some Particular Meetings had been settled in Salisbury's rural hinterland during that decade and that Friends there had developed links with their near neighbours across the county border. Thus, much of the evidence of the early membership and activities of the southern Friends has had to be gleaned from the Dorset registers, although some references to them can be found in the Wiltshire Quarterly

Meeting minutes and the books recording Wiltshire Quakers' 'sufferings' under the Clarendon Code.

The sufferings of south Wiltshire Friends

By refusing to swear oaths, by encouraging the non-payment of tithes, and by refusing to observe conventions in modes of address or behaviour, Quakers were seen as catalysts for widespread resistance to authority.[10] Both Parliament and the Restoration government had reason to suppress such overt displays of dissent, which meant that Quakers frequently found themselves an easy target for communal displeasure. The Restoration government continually tried to clamp down on religious groups meeting outside the established church, key planks in the Clarendon Code being the first Conventicle Act in 1664, and a second more rigorous Conventicle Act in 1670.

At that time, individuals charged with an offence would frequently be held in gaol until they could be tried, rather than as a punishment after a trial, which could mean incarceration for weeks or months before their case was heard. The outcome of the trial might be to levy a fine or to inflict some kind of physical punishment, although subversives convicted under the Clarendon Code increasingly found themselves sentenced to prison terms that could stretch to many years. Once gaoled, inmates were dependent on friends and relatives for support, unless they were wealthy enough to buy in food, drink and bedding, and other essentials to get through their ordeal. The county gaol at Fisherton Anger, near Salisbury was frequently used to hold Quakers from across the whole county while they awaited a court hearing for their alleged offences.

Both sides quickly learned how to use the law to their own advantage, with church officials preferring to use the King's Bench or the Court of Common Pleas rather than the church courts to pursue outstanding tithes as actions of debt against defaulters, since greater penalties could be imposed on those convicted.[11] In 1667 Warminster incumbent Paul Lathorn, exploited the overlapping jurisdictions of the various courts when he sued William Chandler for non-payment of tithes. Initially Lathorn took his claim to the assizes and, when his suit was thrown out there, he transferred his action to the manorial court, where his attorney was a steward. That court was split on the issue, since some felt that they 'ought not to meddle in a case of tythes' but, according to the Friends' account, Lathorn had a private word with some of the jurors, who were thus 'persuaded' to find in his favour. The Friends' report claimed that the only freeholder present had protested that the proceedings were illegal, but nonetheless the court found in Lathorn's favour and he was able to take from Chandler one yoke of oxen, valued at £13, for the tithe demand of £1 7s 2d.[12]

For their part Quakers exploited a loophole in the law, whenever possible, to have cases of non-payment of tithes restricted to the church courts which lacked an effective process to enforce payment, although they still risked being sent to prison on the writ of excommunication.[13] Although magistrates and justices do not appear to have made such distinctions, the Wiltshire Friends differentiated between their 'crimes' and those of other categories of offenders, with Edward Gye of Market Lavington objecting to being incarcerated with those he termed as 'common felons'.[14]

Both men and women could be imprisoned for their actions, and itinerant missionaries ran the risk of harsh treatment as vagrants when apprehended for public preaching. The early movement encouraged capable women preachers such as Katharine Evans of Bath to become missionaries. In 1657 Evans's visit to Salisbury resulted in her being publicly rebuked and then publicly whipped in the market place and her second visit saw her confined to the blind house[15] before being turned out of the city under the Elizabethan vagrancy statutes, to spend the night in the fields.[16] Undeterred Evans enlisted the support of Wiltshire Quaker woman, Sarah Cheevers, and the two set off on a missionary expedition to Alexandria. Their journey was interrupted when they stopped in Malta for some impromptu evangelising and were imprisoned there by the Grand Inquisitor for three and a half years.[17]

The Monthly Meetings regularly arranged visits to Quakers in prison in the county, to give moral support and to provide them with essential supplies until their release could be secured. An example from 1661 serves to demonstrate that these acts of charity could be hazardous undertakings. Four women from the Wiltshire East district, Katharine Saunders, Alice Hellier, Elizabeth Harris and Anne Gerish, made the long journey to visit Friends being held in the county gaol at Fisherton Anger. However, on their arrival they were taken before the Salisbury mayor and also imprisoned, although no specific charge was laid against them.[18] In addition to these well meaning but often thwarted local measures, the wider Quaker community could also provide relief for prisoners suffering financial hardships, such as the generous gift of £5 10s sent by Friends in Ireland for the relief of Friends in prison in Salisbury.[19]

Implementation of the Acts that made up the Clarendon Code was inconsistent, with some magistrates – often at the insistence of local clergy – acting with what now seems like undue harshness, while others took a more relaxed approach to religious dissent. In 1670 the Bishop of Salisbury complained to the Warminster justices that there were 'divers great and outrageous meetings' of dissenters within their district.[20] After making a token investigation, a sympathetic Sir Edward Hungerford and his colleagues informed Bishop Seth Ward that they could not find any such meetings.[21]

Not everyone could afford to follow Hungerford's approach and the fact that Conventicle Acts allowed for a scale of payments to informers created ill feelings in some communities. Motives to inform could be complex, from a genuine desire to stamp out unorthodox religious practises, to acts of revenge against neighbours or business rivals, to good old-fashioned greed. The numbers of arrests increased at times of political crisis, such as the moves between 1679-1681 to exclude James, Duke of York from the succession, and the fears generated by the Popish Plot of 1678 and the Rye House Plot of 1683. The powers wielded, and fear engendered, by some informers are illustrated by the reaction of the Salisbury justices to a plea for clemency from a group of local Quakers. In 1686 George Harris, Robert Shergold and Phillip Pine met with the mayor of Salisbury and several justices 'to perswade them to deal friendly by us; some of them said they would doe us any kindness'.[22] However the informers were 'resolved in their minds to prosecute us to ye utmost they can' and left the justices afraid that they would also be fined if they failed to uphold the letter of the law.[23]

Nevertheless, the pressure began to ease for Quakers and other dissenters with the accession of James II. During his short reign (1685-1688), James granted two Declarations of Indulgence, in 1687 and 1688, in support of religious toleration, in addition to the general pardon he had granted to dissenters in 1685. Under these Declarations all penal laws against the Quakers were immediately suspended.[24]

Toleration and Decline

After suffering decades of persecution of their beliefs the Friends were offered some respite under the Toleration Act of 1689, which allowed them to register certain premises to be used for religious worship outside the established church. In January 1690 the Wiltshire clerk submitted an application to register 22 premises en bloc for use as Quaker meeting houses.[25] Unsurprisingly, since the heartland of the Wiltshire Quaker movement was in the north and west of the county, most of these earliest registrations were for premises in the north, with only five situated in the south. Up to 1707 the Wiltshire Quarterly Meeting's clerk Stephen Jones countersigned the applications for half of the registrations across the county, from Calne in the north to Mere in the south-west. The Friends at Mere in the south-west corner had never had strong ties with the Wiltshire Friends, looking rather to Dorset for support,[26] but they still had to register their meeting house with the Wiltshire justices.

Within three years of the Toleration Act coming into force the Salisbury Friends were feeling more confident that they could meet in the cathedral city without being harassed and so were able to assert their independence from their distant colleagues in central and north Wiltshire.[27] They acquired their own designated meeting house in 1692, although this was not registered as a meeting place for worship until 1703.[28] Having regularised their position they split from the Lavington Monthly Meeting to set up their own Monthly Meeting for the whole of the southern district.[29] Although no minutes of the Salisbury Monthly Meeting survived from this period it can be deduced from the Quarterly

Chart 2: Particular Meetings Affiliated to the Wiltshire Monthly Meetings c.1700

Wilts East/ Charlcutt Monthly Meeting	Chippenham Monthly Meeting	Lavington Monthly Meeting	Sarum/Salisbury Monthly Meeting
Charlcutt	Chippenham	(Market) Lavington	Salisbury
Purton	Brinkworth	Melksham	Fovant
Marlborough	Kington	Bradford	Whaddon
Calne	Slaughterford	Warminster	Stapleford
Bromham	Corsham	Westbury (including Trowbridge)	Alderbury
Devizes			

Meeting minutes that it was supported by the Particular Meetings at Salisbury, Fovant, Whaddon, Stapleford and, for a brief period, Alderbury.

However, the Quarterly Meeting was unhappy with the unauthorised actions of the Salisbury Friends and, although reluctant to insist that the Salisbury Monthly Meeting be disbanded, the minutes noted in 1704 that: 'This Meeting takes notice of it, and is doubtful that the end of their parting with Lavington Monthly Meeting to be a Monthly Meeting of themselves is not answered, and therefore desire that they will take the same into consideration and to joyne again with Lavington Monthly Meeting, if they think fit'.[30]

This vague and woolly statement by the Quarterly Meeting did not deter the Salisbury Friends, who were unwilling to surrender their independence, and at the next Quarterly Meeting Robert Shergold and John Baker responded that Friends 'at Sarum are willing to continue by themselves yet longer'.[31] With the support of the southern Particular Meetings, the Salisbury Monthly Meeting continued for over a decade, thriving well enough to have its own meeting house built in 1712.[32] Ironically, within only a few years, support for the meeting had dwindled to the point where the Stapleford Particular Meeting was omitted from the Quarterly Meeting list in 1715[33] and that at Fovant shortly after. Now rather isolated in the south, and after their brief spell of autonomy, the Salisbury Friends agreed to merge their Monthly Meeting with that at Lavington in 1717.[34]

In 1724 the Quarterly Meeting tried to rationalise membership of the three remaining Monthly Meetings by realigning the affiliations of their Particular Meetings 'to reduce travelling within all the Monthly Meeting divisions'.[35] Initially, the Chippenham Monthly Meeting had unanimously agreed that the Bradford Friends should join their division so that the Salisbury Friends could be better accommodated in the Lavington division.[36] The reassignment of other meetings followed in February 1725. These rearrangements proved generally unpopular and attendance at all the Monthly Meetings fell, so the experiment was quickly abandoned. By October 1725 all Particular Meetings had reverted to their original Monthly Meetings, with the southern meetings once again part of the Lavington division, on the understanding that Salisbury should not host any Monthly Meetings. The Salisbury Friends were given a special dispensation to attend only such Monthly Meetings 'as they found convenient'.[37]

The 18th century saw the rise of Methodism, which proved an attractive alternative to some of the younger Quakers who saw the rules imposed by their parents as old fashioned and restrictive, and this contributed to the fall in Quaker membership. This decline in membership, initially experienced at the Particular and Monthly Meetings, had filtered through to the Quarterly Meeting by the third quarter of the century. In order to remain viable the three remaining Monthly Meetings merged in 1775 to become the Wiltshire Monthly Meeting but, despite the apparent duplication of function, the Wiltshire Quarterly Meeting continued to meet as a separate body for a further ten years. Friends in the neighbouring county of Gloucestershire, with whom the north Wiltshire Quakers had already had strong links by 1740, were experiencing the same difficulties as their Wiltshire counterparts. In 1785 the two county Quarterly Meetings joined together to form the Wiltshire and Gloucester Quarterly Meeting.[38] Salisbury Friends, already remote from the county network, were omitted from this merger. The southern part of the county had long had close links with neighbouring Hampshire so the Salisbury Friends became part of Ringwood Monthly Meeting and the Hampshire Quarterly Meeting.

Conclusion

Quakerism came to south Wiltshire later than to the northern parts of the county and Friends there developed their own networks of support with geographically convenient meetings, rather than following either the county's civil or the Quakers' own administrative set-ups. Nevertheless, these Quakers followed the same codes of practice as their colleagues in the rest of Wiltshire and stood beside them in the face of legal and ecclesiastical challenges to their right to worship as they saw fit. Having come through adversity the Quaker movement gradually declined in numbers, with smaller meetings catering for larger geographical areas, but still survives to this day in both Salisbury and the north of the county.

Salisbury Quakers and their meeting houses, *by Sue Johnson*

By 1680 Salisbury had 'a considerable group, including some prosperous citizens' whose meeting place was Alderbury.[39] A burial place at Whaddon was given by Thomas Elcock in 1688.[40] They presumably continued to meet at Alderbury until 1689 when property in Salisbury was conveyed to trustees 'for the purpose of a meeting house and Burial Ground'.[41] In 1692-3 a minute of the

Wiltshire Quarterly Meeting mentions the 'removing of the Alderbury Meeting to Sarum as they see meet' and shortly afterwards the Salisbury Meeting is referred to as 'resumed'.[42] The location of the meeting house and burial ground acquired in 1692[43] does not appear to be recorded but the suggestion in the 1853 return to Charity Commissioners is that it was always the same site in Gigant Street. In 1699 the house of Thomas Hayward in Fisherton Anger (technically a separate parish, but effectively a suburb of Salisbury) was registered, followed four years later by those of Robert Shergold and John Moore in Salisbury and of John Baker in East Harnham – again no streets are specified.[44] Soon after (1712) a meeting house and burial ground in Gigant Street were opened. Described as 'new built' when it was registered in January 1713 it was certified by Robert Shergold, James Lonsdale, and James Wilkins.[45] No description or illustration of the building has been found, the only information given in later deeds being that there were 2 tenements and a plot of garden ground given by Robert Shergold, on which a meeting house had been built, and that the site measured approximately 73 feet east to west, and 25 feet north to south.[46] The location is shown on 1797 and 1833 town maps.

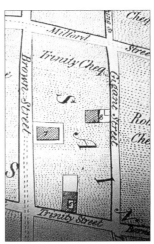

The Gigant Street meeting house, shown as no 8 on the map of Salisbury by G O Lucas, 1833 (WSA G23/1/165)

The exact numbers of Quakers in the city are hard to determine, however some indication is available from surviving sources. When the Gigant Street property was conveyed to new trustees in November 1766 by Joseph Moore, the last survivor of the previous trustees, of the 12 people named only 4 were local – James Pritchard, clothier, Wm Jeffery the younger, miller and Henry Jeffery, druggist, all of Salisbury and Richard Smith the younger, miller, from Fisherton Anger.[47] The answers to Visitation Queries in the diocese of Salisbury in 1783 record the presence of about two dozen Quakers, 21 in St Thomas parish, where the incumbent said that 'Their numbers have not increased according to my observation' and there was no place for their divine worship, or where they assembled. St Martin had a Quaker meeting house but those who attended it mostly came from other parishes, while St Edmund mentioned no Quakers at all, and in Fisherton Anger there were said to be only two or three. At Wilton there were only 'a few' Quakers but a 'great number' of Methodists.[48]

An alphabetical listing of Quaker burials in Wiltshire is given in a series of articles in volumes 5-7 of Wiltshire Notes and Queries. Between 1706 and 1784 there are 6 people described as being of Sarum, with a further 26 burials at Sarum, at least 3 of whom came from Wilton. Included is Robert Shergold of Sarum, 20-11-1717, presumably one of the people named on the Gigant Street certificate. When the *Salisbury Journal* of 9 June 1788 recorded the marriage at the Meeting House of John Sanger, of Cirencester, to Lydia Smith daughter of Richard Smith, coal-merchant of Fisherton, it noted that it was 'the only ceremony of the kind that has been celebrated in this city for near 40 years.' As numbers dwindled the Gigant Street building fell into disuse, possibly as early as 1796.[49] Alternative venues in the city had been registered – the houses of Martin Neave and Joseph Moore as usual plus that of James Moore in Castle St, Salisbury, for occasional use, in December 1760, and 'large room' in William Fricker's house, in Salt Lane, in July 1787.[50] When Deborah Darby of Coalbrookdale visited the city in 1799 and 1800 public meetings were held at the Assembly Rooms, the second occasion being described by her as a 'large and solemn' meeting. [51]

Because of its 'weak state' the Salisbury Meeting was discontinued in 1826 and its books removed to Southampton.[52] In March of that year 'A building in Gigant St in St Martin's parish heretofore used as a place of worship by Quakers' was registered as an Independent meeting house.[53] The building eventually became an Infant School, the draft lease, dated 29 July 1830, reserving the right for the Quakers to hold occasional religious meetings in the building.[54] Following the closure of the school the meeting house was let to the Temperance Society in 1876. It was sold to them the following year for £225 and the money used for the rebuilding and enlargement of the Meeting House at Newport, Isle of Wight.[55] The site was eventually engulfed by the Anchor Brewery. Graves disturbed during work on the brewery buildings and redevelopment of the site after its closure were no doubt from the burial ground belonging to the Meeting house.[56]

Any surviving Salisbury Friends presumably continued to meet in private houses, but by 1854 the return to Charity Commissioners notes that there was then 'No Friend resident in the Neighbourhood to keep open the Meeting.'[57] In 1889 an attempt was made by Alfred Cook to get a meeting place in Salisbury for the eight or nine Friends and attenders resident in the city, who were going to Wilton to join the three or four Friends there. Meetings were held for a time in his house, but following a disagreement about whether there should or should not be a separate meeting at Salisbury he discontinued these in the following year. Possible venues included a return to the original meeting house

Kennet Lodge, 2003. Photograph by Hugh Teed

in Gigant Street, or a room in Castle Street, but after consultation with Salisbury Friends all but Alfred Cook and his wife were in favour of continuing to go to Wilton[58] and proposals for a separate meeting place in Salisbury seem to have been abandoned.

In the 1920s meetings were held in the house of Charles and Florence Dingle[59] and ten years later (1934) the Salisbury Meeting re-opened in hired rooms at the Rechabite Hall in Crane Street.[60] It was almost another 30 years before Salisbury Friends again had their own meeting place when in 1962 a house at 44 Rectory Road was purchased. A derelict building on the Old Manor Hospital site, called Kennet Lodge, was acquired in 2003 and the slow process of raising funds to refurbish it to provide a modern multi-functional venue began. The builders moved on site in October 2009 and completed their task in April 2010, with the first meeting for worship held there on May 2 – a welcome landmark after several years spent in a variety of hired rooms.

Work in progress, October 2009. Photograph by Hugh Teed

Notes and References

At the Dorset History Centre [DRO]
DRO File NQ2 Register of Dorset Friends' Births 1648-1836
DRO File NQ3 Register of Dorset Friends' Burials 1659-1836;
DRO File NQ4 Register of Dorset Friends' Marriages 1668-1836.
NQ1/19/2-6 Deeds relating to meeting houses and burial grounds at various places including Salisbury, 1830-46

At the Wiltshire and Swindon History Centre [WSA]
WSA 854/14 List of Places used by the People of God called Quakers for the Purpose of Religious Worship that may be Recorded According to the Late Act of Parliament, 1689-1716.
WSA 1699/17 A Collection of the Sufferings of the People called Quakers in Wiltshire from the year 1653 [to 1702].
WSA 1699/31 Sarum/South Wiltshire Monthly Meeting Minute Book 1704-17.

WSA 1699/37 Minutes of the Wiltshire Monthly Meeting and the Gloucester and Wiltshire Quarterly Meeting, with miscelleneous notes 1810-1872.

WSA 1699/38 The Memorial of the Quarterly Meetings of the People of God called Quakers, in the Countie of Wilts. 1678-1708.

WSA 1699/40 Minutes of the Quarterly Meetings of Wiltshire Friends 1708-1734.

WSA 1699/75 Wiltshire East (Charlcote) Monthly Meetings Minute Book 1677-1705.

WSA 854/76 Lavington Monthly Meeting Minute Book 1692-1774.

WSA 1699/79 Chippenham Monthly Meetings Minute Book 1669-1709.

WSA 1699/80 Chippenham Monthly Meetings Minutes 1714-1725.

WSA 854/83 Counsel's opinions and legal papers.

At Hampshire Record Office [HRO]

24M54/95 Poole & Ringwood Monthy Meeting 1825-30

24M54/306/6 Copy return for 1853 made to Charity Commissioners about Charities belonging to the Society of Friends, dated 13-5mo-1854

24M54/337/1-22 Correspondence concerning a place of meeting at Salisbury. 1889-91

24M54/338/1-6 Deeds relating to Whaddon Burial Ground, Wilts, for the Salisbury Meeting 1668-1788 (item 5 relates to Salisbury Meeting House)

Secondary sources

Barber, Bruno. The Development of Trinity Chequer: Excavations at the Anchor Brewery Site, Giant Street, Salisbury in *WANHM*, 2005, 165-212

Brailsford, Mabel R (1915) *Quaker Women 1650-1690*. London: Duckworth.

Braithwaite, William C (1918, 1979) *The Second Period of Quakerism*. York: Sessions.

Butler, David M (1) (1999) *The Quaker Meeting Houses of Britain* vol 2.

London: Friends Historical Society.

Butler, David M (2), Meeting Houses Built and Meetings Settled. Answers to Yearly Meeting Queries 1688-1791. *Journal of the Friends Historical Society*, Vol 51, 1965-1967, p174-211.

Chandler, John H (1985) *Wiltshire Dissenters' Meeting House Certificates and Registrations 1689-1852*. Gloucester: WRS vol 40

Fassnidge, Harold (1992) *The Quakers of Melksham 1669-1950*. Wiltshire: Bradford-on-Avon Friends.

Goldney, Frederick H (1889) *Records of Chippenham 1554-1889*. London: Diprose.

Green, Mary A E (editor) (1895), *Calendar of State Papers Domestic, 1670 with addenda 1660 to 1670*. London: HMSO.

Greenwood, John Max (1994) 'Quakers in the Devizes Area - a Survey of 340 Years of History'. Wiltshire: typescript [copy at WSA].

Hemming, Alan, Copy of typescript notes on the History of Quakers in Salisbury prepared for a meeting on 23-5-1996

Hill, Christopher (1972) *The World Turned Upside Down*. London: Penguin

Horle, Craig W (1988) *The Quakers and the English Legal System 1660-1688*. Philadelphia: Pennsylvania State University Press.

Kegl, Rosemary (1995) 'Women's Preaching, Absolute Property, and the Cruel Sufferings (for the truths sake) of Katharine Evans and Sarah Chevers'. *Women's Studies (Great Britain)*, vol 24, no 1-2, 51-83.

Labouchere, Rachel, *Deborah Darby of Coalbrookdale 1754-1810*. William Sessions Ltd, 1993

Nuttall, G F and Chadwick, O (1962), *From Uniformity to Unity*, London: SPCK.

Penney, Norman (1898) 'Sufferers for Conscience Sake'. *Wiltshire Notes and Queries* vol 2, 163-183.

Pope, Dr. Walter (1697) *The Life of the Right Reverend Father in God,*

Seth Lord Bishop of Salisbury and Chancellor of the most Noble Order of the Garter, written by Dr Walter Pope of the Royal Society. London

Powell, W R (1952) 'The Society of Friends in Wiltshire'. *Journal of the Friends Historical Society* vol 44, 3-10.

Ransome, Mary (ed), *Returns to Visitation Queries, 1783*. WRS vol 27, 1972

Reay, Barry (1980) 'Quaker Opposition to Tithes, 1652-1660'. *Past and Present*, vol 86, 198-120.

Reay, Barry (1980) 'Popular Hostility towards Quakers in mid-Seventeenth-Century England', *Social History*, vol 5, 387-407.

Smith, William (1982) 'A Select Account of the Private Papers of Bishop Seth Ward in the Wiltshire Record Office'. *WANHM* vol 76, 115-122.

Whitehead, John (1661) *A Small Treatise*.

Whiteman, Anne (1962) 'The Restoration of the Church of England', in G F Nuttall and O Chadwick (eds), *From Uniformity to Unity*, London: SPCK.

VCH Wiltshire, volume 3, 1956, 117-119

VCH Wiltshire, volume 6, 1962, 157

Salisbury Times 8 June 1962, p5, item on meeting house in Rectory Rd [STM]

Salisbury Quakers website www.salisbury-quakers.co.uk

1   This paper draws on the research for my PhD thesis: Taylor, Kay S (2006) Society, Schism and Sufferings: The First 70 Years of Quakerism in Wiltshire. Bristol: University of the West of England. To find out more about Quaker beliefs visit www.quaker.org.uk

2   Whitehead

3   Reay (Tithes), 101 and Reay (Hostility), 391.

4   Smith, 115-122.

5   WSA 1699/79 and WSA 1699/75

6   WSA 1699/38

7   WSA 854/76

8   WSA 1699/31

9   DRO Files NQ2, NQ3 and NQ4

10   Reay (Tithes), 101.

11   Horle, 54; and Whiteman, 111, have demonstrated that the episcopal administration was not in full working order until 1663.

12   WSA 1699/17 entry dated 5mo 1667. (Quakers refused to use names for months but referred to them by number starting in March, so 5mo = July)

13   Horle, 53.

14   WSA 1699/17 entry dated 6mo 1663.

15   Many Wiltshire towns made use of a 'blind house'. This was a small windowless cell, commonly used to confine drunkards overnight until they sobered up. It also used to detain troublemakers before either taking them before the magistrate or escorting them out of town.

16   WSA 1699/17 entry dated 24 5mo 1658. Although the book of sufferings dates Evans' offences to 1658, it would appear that the incidents referred to actually occurred in late 1657, prior to Evans and Cheevers going to London to prepare for their trip to Alexandria. See also Hill, 49.

17   Brailsford, 207 208; and Kegl, 59.

18   WSA 1699/17 entry dated 5mo 1661.

19   1699/38 entry dated 29 10mo 1684.

20   Green, 424, entry dated 22 September 1670.

21   Ibid, 448, entry dated 22 September 1670. Goldney, 328, lists Sir Edward Hungerford as being returned as MP for Chippenham in the late 1670s.

22   WSA 1699/17 entry dated 29 7mo 1686.

23   Ibid and Penney, 176-177. See also WSA 854/83. A justice could be fined £100 for refusing to grant a properly requested warrant.

24   Braithwaite, 130.

25   WSA 854/14 and Chandler, item 24.

26   Powell, 10

27   Smith, 116, recounted the reputation of Bishop of Salisbury, Seth Ward (1667-1689) for assiduously persecuting Dissenters. Smith also noted that Ward's biographer, Walter Pope, had reported that, under James II, Ward had been 'enjoined to moderate

his zeal and not Molest Dissenters.'
However, Smith was not convinced
of Pope's accuracy and suggested that
his account of Ward's actions against
Nonconformists was an exaggeration.

28 Butler, 687; and Chandler, item 135.
29 WSA 854/76
30 WSA 1699/38   entry dated 3 2mo
    1704.
31 Ibid, entry dated 3 5mo 1704.
32 WSA 1699/38 ; Fassnidge, 117; and
    Butler, 687.
33 WSA 1699/40 entry dated 2 11mo
    1715.
34 WSA 1699/31   entry dated 10 May
    1717.
35 WSA 1699/40 entry dated 10mo
    1724.
36 WSA 1699/80 entry dated 18 11mo
    1724.
37 Greenwood, 5, 14; and WSA 1699/40
    various entries for 1725.
38 WSA 1699/37. There are no extant
    minutes for the joint Quarterly Meeting
    for the period 1785-1810.
39 VCH 3, p117
40 HRO 24M54/338/1
41 HRO 24M54/306/6
42 Hemming/VCH3, 118
43 Butler (1), 687
44 Chandler, items 73, 135
45 Butler (1), 687; Chandler, item 192
46 HRO 24M54/338/5
47 DRO NQ1/19/2
48 Ransome, items 200, 137, 79, 84, 217
49 Butler (2), 194
50 Chandler, items 313, 397
51 Labouchere, 255, 269. Neither event
    is reported in the Salisbury Journal
52 VCH 6, 157; HRO 24M54/95, entries
    for   4-11mo-1825,   6-1mo-1826,
    3-2mo-1826
53 Chandler, item 693
54 DRO NQ1/R19/3
55 Butler (1) 687; HRO 24M54/222, 43,
    77, 82, 86, 90-91, 131
56 STM 1962; Barber 181-2
57 HRO 24M54/306/6
58 HRO 24M54/337/1-22
59 Hemming
60 STM 1962

*The completed building in Wilton Road. Designed by Philip Proctor Associates and
built by Spetisbury Construction, the project cost about half a million pounds*

A Century of Girl Guiding in the Salisbury area: some events from the first 60 years

Maureen Davidson

The popularity of the Boy Scout Movement, founded in 1907 by Lord Baden-Powell, soon led to demands for a similar organisation for girls. His sister, Agnes Baden-Powell, was asked to organise it and by 1910 a separate Girl Guide Movement with 6000 members had been established. Agnes compiled a handbook for Girl Guides, called *How Girls can help to Build up the Empire,* which was published in 1912. Early badges included First Aid, Cyclist, Nurse, Electrician, Tailor, Clerk and Telegraphist. Olave, Lord Baden-Powell's wife, was enrolled as a Girl Guide in 1915 and by 1918 was Chief Commissioner. She retained this office until her death in 1977, supporting the Guide Movement with great enthusiasm.

Salisbury was not long in joining the new organisation and in 1911 Miss Baden-Powell, a friend of Miss E M Stevens, the Captain of the first Girl Guide Company in Salisbury, was invited to Salisbury to enrol its first members. She was met at the railway station by the 1st Salisbury Company and escorted to the Maundrel Hall in Fisherton Street where the Guides made their Promises. The first Patrol was called the Sunflowers and the first Guide, Gwendoline Miles, designed and embroidered the Patrol Flag.[1] The Company, until it was suspended (about 2000 – no record exists of the exact date), always had a Sunflower Patrol.

Guiding grew slowly in the Salisbury area. When Lady Baden-Powell visited the newly formed Salisbury and District Association of Girl Guides in the spring of 1918 she remarked that 'It had apparently taken six years for the movement to be understood in Salisbury'. Six months earlier there had only been one Company, under Miss Stevens, now there there were 5 in the city and one at Alderbury.[2] By June when about 300 Guides from the city and other parts of the county attended a rally in the grounds of Llangarren, Wilton Road, it was stated that the number of Guides in the county had more than trebled in the past year. Those present included the 1st, 2nd, 3rd, 5th and 6th Salisbury,

1st Alderbury and 1st Wilton Guides, and the 1st Salisbury Brownies. There were assorted demonstrations including drill by the 1st Salisbury Guides and signalling by the 2nd Salisbury.[3]

The Alderbury Company was started in November 1911 by Lady Elizabeth Pleydell-Bouverie, or Lady Betty, as she was affectionately known. Together with her sisters she took part in a highly successful concert given by the Alderbury and Salisbury Companies at the Assembly Rooms, Salisbury, on 4 December 1912. The programme, which with other matters relating to the concert, was arranged by Miss Stevens, included the Guides performing 'the song and march of the Baden-Powell Guides' and the 'Song of the Salisbury Guides'. In the interval Lady Muriel Herbert explained the Guide Movement to the large audience.[4]

The Senior Section for older girls began in 1916, and was renamed as Rangers in 1920. Kathleen Speck, born in 1909, was a member of a Ranger Unit attached to St Edmund's Church, Salisbury and recalled that the Rector's wife wrote plays, particularly for Christmas. The Rangers played the Angels and wore long nightdresses with silver tinsel around their heads. They had to say 'This is the Light of the World' and a light came on. A side chapel had been screened off as a dressing room and after the play a choir boy came and asked Kathleen to see the Rector before she went home. She wondered what she had done wrong. The Rector said, 'May I present you with the light of the World?' It was Kathleen's bicycle lamp. Before the play started the church lights had partially fused and at the suggestion of one of the choir boys the lamp had been placed under the straw and used instead.[5]

Not long after the foundation of the Guides came the outbreak of the First World War. Local Guides helped the war effort in various ways including collecting waste paper and taking round papers in connection with War Bond Week.[6] A very special service was rendered to Sergeant H J Roper of the Canadian Infantry, whose letter was read out at the Girl Guide Commissioners Conference at Swanwick in 1918:

> Dear Miss,
> Will you find out one of your young lady officers and give her the enclosed and thanks for me? I should have been a goner last night but for her. Being still a bit dazed and deaf from shell shock I was going to Victoria after a bite at the ABC at the corner and never saw or heard two taxis coming straight at me.
>
>   Miss I felt a dash behind me, and this young lady officer must have run direct in front of both motors and grabbed my arm and pulled me quick across to the safe kerb…. And the motors were coming quick and one caught her … something terrible hard on her shoulder… She only stayed to see I was right and wouldn't stay for no thanks – said she was a guide.

On 25 August 1918 at Swanwick Lady Baden-Powell decorated Miss Marjorie Storey, Commissioner for Salisbury, with the Silver Cross for Gallantry.[7]

In 1925 the 5th Salisbury Guides knitted scarves and gloves and made woollen balls and toys to send to children in the village of Hanley, near St Quenton, in France. An Amesbury Company passed on the idea after there was a request in the local paper to 'adopt' children of devastated villages in France. A grateful letter of thanks was received from the village schoolmaster.[8]

A more enjoyable event occurred in 1924 when a Brownie Rally was held on Empire Day (24 May). When first formed in 1914 the junior section for Guides under 11 were called 'Rosebuds', changing to the current name a year later. Scheduled to be held in the grounds of the Bishop's Palace, the Close, Salisbury, the rally was transferred to the Wesleyan Hall due to very wet weather. Over 130 Brownies attended and the Packs marched around and were inspected by the Assistant County Commissioner Lady Congreve. The Brownies also took part in action songs and performed plays, followed by a Treasure Hunt. After tea, each received a small present and the National Anthem was sung to conclude the afternoon.[9]

In 1932 Lady Baden-Powell came to Salisbury Cathedral for a Guide Service. The Chief sat with the Guides and, as she got up, caught her heel in the hem of her skirt. One Guide had her 'hussif' [sewing kit] and after being allowed to repair the hem had her note book signed by Lady Baden-Powell.[10]

Going to camp has always been an integral Guiding activity, but it was not easy in the early days. A Guide from the 1st Salisbury Company borrowed her kit and went to Salisbury railway station hoping to join a camp near Devizes. She waited for a guard to let her travel free, with her bicycle, in his van, as she had the cost of the camp but not the rail fare. If she did not manage this she returned home and tried again the next day. She eventually got her wish and from Devizes Railway Station she cycled to the camp in her uniform, with her equipment, flag and pole. After the camp the reverse happened and she waited at Devizes railway station for another kindly guard to let her travel to Salisbury. It is not recorded how long the return journey took![11]

Barbara Ryrie, a member of Sarum Trefoil Guild, remembered making palliases – hessian sacks filled with straw used as camp mattresses. The farmer where you camped would sell you straw for a few pence. The straw all went to one end when you slept on it, she recalled, so you ended up either with your feet in the air and your head down, or the other way round. When folded up in a groundsheet for day time to keep them dry, they were like the huge bales now seen at harvest time.[12]

In the Summer of 1924 1st West Lavington Guides went to camp in a crowded lorry to Wilton Park, (the grounds of Wilton House) an hour's drive away. The camp took place by kind permission of the Countess of Pembroke. Eight different companies were in camp and the West Lavington Guides became the Thistle Patrol, very appropriate as the camp site was covered in thistles.[13] Many early County Camps took place at Wilton Park, and the 5th Salisbury log book reports that full uniform was worn for breakfast (see also cover illustration). Two cricket matches were arranged, one against the Wolf Cubs, who won 16 runs to 9, and the second against Wilton House whose team included the County Commissioner, Lady Pembroke. The ball hit by the County Commissioner ended up in the river but the Guides were beaten 83 runs to 47.[14]

The Hobnobs of the 5th Salisbury Company washing up during their camp in Wilton Park between the wars

At camp in 1933 in Devon 5th Salisbury Rangers found a dog had taken their bacon (worth 2 shillings and 6 pence) and 14 fish cakes. Some Rangers had to leave the camp early to return home to work and missed the bus to Exeter. They hitched a lift and by mistake took one of the driver's parcels as well as their own when they left his car. They took the parcel to the Police and this caused many 'Girl Guide' jokes and merriment. The parcel eventually arrived back with its owner.[15]

1st 'A' Amesbury Rangers camped for the weekend near the Bustard Inn, Shrewton in 1937 – some travelled to camp by bicycle. Presumably the camp equipment went separately. Washing took place in the animal trough in the field and there is mention of a wind-up gramophone being taken.[16]

Joan Pine was in camp when the Second World War broke out and the Police told the camp to return home. After the Guides had left the Guiders returned home by car, at night, and only side lights were allowed. On the way home they called into a Bed and Breakfast establishment in Blandford and asked for just breakfast – no bed required. It is to be hoped this request was granted![17]

Camping continued during the Second World War, though sites had to be local. The only thing which seemed to limit it was a serious outbreak of foot and mouth disease in 1942. War time food rationing meant everyone was asked to take some food to camp (the items were added to the kit list) and leftovers were shared out. One Guider recalled cycling home with a not quite set bowl of dripping, luckily a short trip from the camp site. At harvest time rabbits were caught, skinned and cooked.

Guides aided the war effort in various ways. At a camp at Broadchalke, near Salisbury, the 10th and 12th Salisbury Guides assisted with farm work. Whiteparish Guides helped with the collection of 24 hundredweights (1219kg) of paper and light iron.[18] Many items were collected during the war, including hips and nettles for medicines, books for the troops, cotton reels for the Army, and ship halfpennies to buy books for sailors. The 1st Salisbury Guides heard the appeal on the wireless for Scouts and Guides to collect cotton reels and duly organised this. They cycled with their collection to Homington, to deliver them to the Dowager Countess of Radnor, who was acting as the collecting point for the area. On their return journey they visited Odstock Church and one of the Guides accidentally slipped and pulled the bell rope. The sound of the bells was a sign of an invasion but luckily no one heard! In 1941 the Captain and ten Guides from 1st Salisbury Company, in co-operation with St Martin's and St Francis Guides, assisted the Home Guard in an exercise lasting two and a half hours. They were sent a letter of commendation for their participation.[19]

Although the 1st Salisbury's Guide meetings continued during the War they had to be held in a very small room and the meeting had to be split for two years as the normal hall was used as an evacuation Reception Centre where evacuees slept and were fed until billeted. The 1st Salisbury Guides also helped at the YMCA Canteen and at the evacuation centre. Salisbury Guiders helped run the YWCA in the town (situated in the High Street). Joyce Wotton, ex Guider in Charge at Foxlease (the Girl Guide Training Centre at Lyndhurst) was the manager. The Guiders of Salisbury helped cook and wash up. The Centre was eventually

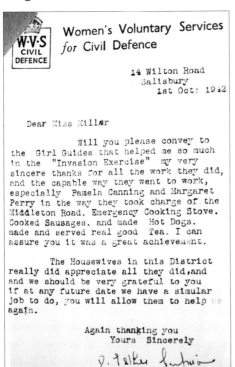

1st Salisbury Company praised for assisting a Home Guard exercise, 1942

moved to the Guide Hut in the Close, Salisbury, and this was used by the ATS and later the WRNS. The Ranger unit at the Salisbury Teachers' Training College, which had existed since about 1928, offered to help on the domestic side of Salisbury Infirmary and worked on a rota system. Sixteen hours were covered each weekend.[20]

Once the war was over camping further afield could resume. From the 1940s onwards the 1st Alderbury Guides made many visits with Dimps Stevens to camp on the Isles of Scilly. A later visit to the Isles of Scilly by the 1st Alderbury Company in 1966 enabled them to obtain the autograph of the then Prime Minister Harold Wilson, who had a holiday home there.

At Freshwater Bay Camp in 1945 two Guides from 1st Salisbury ran away and reached their homes on the second day. After camp at the next Guide meeting it was decided that these two must renew their Promise and apologise to the Camp Commandant.[21] The 1st Alderbury Guides camped at Norton Green on the Isle of Wight in 1948 and: 'The hurricane on the Saturday night will never be forgotten – especially by those of us who had to pitch a tent in the dark and hold on for dear life! Nor shall we forget the Luton Guides who ate our sausages! Or the amusing vicar who came to supper or the Scout Camp fire which never burned!'[22]

On 17-18 June 1946 Salisbury District held a Handicraft Competition which involved 13 Companies, and 9 Brownie, Ranger and Cadet Units. Miss Ellaby, Division Commissioner at the time, said that handwork was a special part of Guide Training. It helped to bring together hand and brain, and no Guide could be first class unless she could use both. Owing to War conditions many of the younger generation found great difficulty in concentrating and the development of some form of handicraft was a great help in encouraging it.[23]

Handicrafts were just one way to earn badges – a task that did not always go smoothly. Pat Macey, once a member of Ist Pewsey Company, recalled her Queen's Guide badge test in the 1950s. She had many challenges including dealing with a person who was unconscious and had cut her wrists. Pat failed the test because she used her own First Aid kit to bind the wounds and not the tea towels in the tester's kitchen. In later years she became a Casualty Sister. Shirley Cole, a 1st Chilmark Guide in 1965 remembered taking her Dairymaid Badge, part of which was to hand and machine milk a cow. 'I lived at Fovant and cycled to Wyatt's Farm, where they had their own dairy, to learn milking. Two brothers of the farmer handed me a shovel and I was instructed to watch out when the cows lifted their tails and to catch the cowpat on my shovel, as this is what they did when I was not there. All went well until two cows lifted their tails at the same time and I got into a bit of a mess!' There is no record of whether she passed this Badge.

Shirley also took her Local History Badge in 1967: 'I knew an elderly lady in Fovant had been in the employ of Queen Victoria. So I put a letter through her door asking if she could tell me about her time as a Victorian maid. Next thing we knew she came to our front door, waving her walking stick and very irate she was, as it turned out that she had been lady in waiting to Queen Victoria'.[24]

Much fundraising for good causes has gone on over the years, for example the £10 15s raised by the 1st Salisbury Company for the Lynmouth disaster in 1952.[25] In 1970 there was a Three Cheers County Challenge and the 1st Amesbury Pack raised £20 towards a wheel chair for a child in the local hospital. The 1st Tisbury Pack raised money for treatment of a blind girl with leprosy (2 years treatment could provide a cure). A sponsored Silence in the same year held by 1st and 2nd Boscombe Down Packs raised £21 for a retired couple to go on holiday in response to Wiltshire County Opportunity Knocks – Lend a Hand Venture.[26]

The post-war years saw many rallies, conferences and official visits. In July 1950 the 13th World Girl Guiding Conference was held at Oxford. Scrolls of Friendship were carried throughout the British Isles to send messages of Friendship to visiting delegates there. Each area was linked to a country and Wiltshire was linked to Egypt. With the Scroll was a book for every Guide member who took part in delivering it to sign. A log book detailing the journeys of the Scrolls was handed to the assigned delegate. Numerous methods of transport for the Scroll in Wiltshire included horse, bicycle, car, runners, walkers and by water. Ist Alderbury Guides paddled across their local river. The Scroll

1st Alderbury Company conveying the Scroll of Friendship by bicycle, 1950

'rested' in various places including Breamore Church and was admired on its journey by American tourists at Stonehenge. At Old Sarum Brownies carried it across to the site of the old Cathedral.[27]

When Lady Baden-Powell came to a County Rally in Salisbury on 19 June 1955 she intended to speak to everyone in the Bishop's Palace grounds but rain drove her into the Cathedral Cloisters. She had to make six speeches in different areas of the Cloisters to include everyone – no sophisticated amplification in those days![28] At a service at Salisbury Cathedral which took place on 16 June 1968 Lady Baden-Powell likened the Guide Movement to a cathedral and told her listeners that 'You are building a structure of good and you are making this world a happier and better place in which to live.' One ex-Guider recalled the thrill of seeing the Chief Guide and remembers not hearing a word that was said in the Cathedral or seeing much. The Brownies stood on their chairs at the end of the service, as the flags and standards were paraded out, and one said 'It looks like the flags are walking by themselves'.[29] In 1970 South Wiltshire held a Diamond Jubilee Dinner at the Red Lion Hotel, Salisbury on 24 April. This was attended by Mrs Gervais Clay, younger daughter of Lord and Lady Baden-Powell. She revealed that the Guides of South Africa had given her mother a £2000 diamond, which was to be sold and the money used for a bursary for Guides overseas travel.[30]

In June 1975 the World Conference of Girl Guides and Girl Scouts was held at Sussex University. Meg Pousty, Wiltshire County Commissioner, who lived in Wilton, attended the conference, and the 1st, 10th and 14th Salisbury Guides visited for the day, changing into their uniforms on the coach. An unusual form of communication was used to send greetings to the Guides in the UK from those attending from other countries – pigeon post. The message for the South West Region arrived in Mr Jarvis' pigeon loft at Coombe Bissett, near Salisbury.[31]

Following their formation in October 1947 Salisbury Sea Rangers in 1948 took the name of SRS Crusader. This was also the name of their boat which was launched by Miss De Beaumont (County Coxswain of Wiltshire and an early Guide who reputedly attended the Boy Scout Rally at Crystal Palace in 1909) and blessed by the Bishop of Salisbury. The dedication of the burgee (triangular flag bearing colours) took place in the Morning Chapel of Salisbury Cathedral in 1952.

Rangers also experienced the joys and perils of going to camp. In 1950 the County Ranger Adventure Camp was held in Savernake Forest. Salisbury Sea Rangers reported catching a bus to Burbage and, having been warned to walk the last six miles, walked nine! Eventually they reached Shalbourne Manor House where Miss De Beaumont and Miss Arkell were waiting. The tents were pitched and supper prepared. At 5.50am on Sunday the Rangers were woken to a cry of 'Strike and pack up camp' and were then directed to reach a signpost where other clues would be found. The records note that 'Somehow instructions never seem to sink in properly when one is half asleep'. Salisbury Rangers were apparently not very good at observing tracking signs but managed to decipher the codes. Eventually they had to pitch camp and cook breakfast. 'We chose a very windy spot and suffered in silence'. After breakfast, camp was struck and they returned to Shalbourne Manor through fields and lanes. On arriving back their lunch included the peas that had been soaked overnight and carried all over the countryside. After lunch they were instructed in the art of harnessing a cart horse by a local farmer and then climbed into the cart and were taken for a ride to the farm he owned. All in all an exciting weekend.

The following year Salisbury Sea Rangers spent a weekend on SRS Hampshire in Poole Harbour. They travelled by bus to Mitchell's Yard and faced a pier which had planks about three feet wide and of six inch intervals, supported by wooden 'stilts' of uneven height. SRS Hampshire was reported as small and in need of painting. Later more crew arrived and had to paddle over mud as the tide had gone out. To obtain water two bins were lowered into a dinghy by means of ropes, then rowed to the jetty water tap for filling. One Ranger stated 'Water flowed down the waist of my bell-bottoms and dampened my enthusiasm'.

In 1958 Salisbury Sea Rangers went to Dartmouth Naval College for the weekend to a regatta. They stayed at the Naval College and practised on the Saturday morning, with races taking place in the afternoon. The Rangers were second in the sealed orders race and Margaret Munt and Anne Salter were third in the Guiders race.[32] By 1967 6th Salisbury Senior Branch Unit had over 30 members in the Land, Sea and Air Rangers and Cadets. They met in Brown Street Baptist Church Hall and Elaine Harrison recalled making, from scratch, a canoe (a kit was bought which contained wood, canvas, glue and pins). Whether it proved to be a seaworthy craft is not recorded.[33]

Lighter moments were provided by events such as the Pancake Races of February 1971, attended by the 6th Salisbury Rangers at Old Sarum, which had a theme of Pancakes through the ages. The overall prize was a mini frying pan for the team with the most marks.[34]

Since 1910 millions of girls and women have been influenced by the Girl Guide Movement, which still remains, at the choice of the girls, a single sex organisation. Guides today enjoy a wide range of activities and challenges and the opportunities to travel further afield. They can still work for traditional badges like Camper, Craft, Cook and First Aid or modern ones such as Circus Skills, Outdoor Pursuits and Performing Arts. The programme may have changed over the years but the original ethos is still evident, with members in over 145 countries.

All Members of the Guide Movement look forward to renewing their promises at 20.10 on 20 October 2010, to celebrate 100 years of the Guides. Long may it continue.

Sources

www.girlguiding.org.uk: the official Guide
    website

At the Wiltshire & Swindon History Centre
WSA 2777/360/20 1st Salisbury Company,
    Log Book, 1929-1947
WSA 2777/360/21 1st Salisbury Company,
    Log Book, 1947-1952
WSA 2777/360/22 1st Salisbury Company,
    Log Book, 1952-1964
WSA 2777/360/23 1st Salisbury Company,
    Log Book, 1965-1980
WSA 2777/360/1 5th Salisbury Company, Log
    Book and photograph album, 1922-1929
WSA 2777/338/13 1st West Lavington
    Company, Log Book with photographs,
    newscuttings and pamphlets, 1924-
    1928
WSA 2777/300/3 1st Amesbury Guides,
    Log book 1937-1950 with leaflets and
    photos
WSA 2777/309/3 1st Bemerton Company,
    Photograph Album with certificates
    and printed material of camps,
    carnivals and parades, 1944-1967
WSA 2777/300/1 Scrapbook of the
    history of the Guide Movement by 1st
    Alderbury Company, c1980
WSA 2777/360/29 5th Salisbury Ranger
    Company, Log Book, 1933
WSA 2777/360/7 6th Salisbury Ranger
    Guide Service Unit, Log Book, 1966-
    1968
WSA 2777/360/9 6th Salisbury Ranger
    Guide Service Unit, Log Book, 1970-
    1972
WSA 2777/500/3 1918 Girl Guide
    Gazette with article about gallantry
    by Miss Storey, Commissioner for
    Salisbury, and miscellaneous papers
WSA 2777/105/1 Annual Reports 1963-
    1976

Others
Sea Rangers log books, 1950s onwards
    held by Margaret Munt
When I was a Guide – Memories of Sarum
    Trefoil Guild 2003, compiled by Elaine
    Harrison [no page numbers]

A tape recording by Joan Pine, member
    of the Girl Guide Association, now
    deceased [Made in her home on
    29/4/88 and held by Maureen
    Davidson]

Notes

*Salisbury Times [ST]   Salisbury Journal
    [SJL]*

1   Tape recording. The exact founding
    date of the 1st Salisbury Company
    has proved elusive as it was not given
    on the tape, and the author has been
    unable to track down early records.
2   ST 1918, Mch 08, p2
3   ST 1918, Jne 14, p2
4   WSA 2777/360/20; SJL 1912, Dec 7,
    p7
5   *When I was a Guide*
6   ST 1918, Mch 08, p2
7   WSA 2777/500/3
8   WSA 2777/360/1
9   WSA 2777/360/1
10 Tape recording
11 WSA 2777/360/20
12 *When I was a Guide*
13 WSA 2777/338/13
14 WSA 2777/338/13
15 WSA 2777/360/29
16 WSA 2777/300/3
17 Tape recording
18 ST 1941, Dec 05, p8
19 WSA 2777/360/20
20 WSA 2777/360/20
21 WSA 2777/360/20
22 WSA 2777/300/1
23 WSA 2777/360/1
24 *When I was a Guide*
25 WSA 2777/360/22
26 WSA 2777/105/1
27 WSA 2777/309/3
28 WSA 2777/360/22
29 WSA 2777/360/23
30 WSA 2777/105/1
31 WSA 2777/105/1
32 Sea Rangers log books
33 WSA 2777/360/7
34 WSA 2777/360/9

Salisbury's Aesthetic Sunflowers
Richard Deane and John Elliott

The aesthetic movement of the 19th century took as its motif the sunflower. This paper will attempt to assess the impact of the movement on Salisbury by considering the extent to which such motifs can be found in the city's suburbs. Oscar Wilde considered that

> Aesthetics are higher than ethics. They belong to a more spiritual sphere. To discern the beauty of a thing is the finest point to which we can arrive ... Aesthetics, in fact, are to Ethics in the sphere of conscious civilization, what, in the sphere of the external world, sexual is to natural selection. Ethics, like natural selection, make existence possible. Aesthetics, like sexual selection, make life lovely and wonderful, fill it with new forms, and give it progress, and variety and change.[1]

The key to aestheticism was its rejection of contemporary society, and of an art ethos that was derived from, or depended upon, the industrial process. Like the earlier Pre-Raphaelite art form, aestheticism was "lived-out" as a part of life, where its followers could arrange every aspect of their surroundings – architecture, wall coverings, furniture, crockery, textiles and art – as well as hairstyles and clothing to announce their adherence to its principles. An essential element was a redefinition of what constituted female beauty with the most typical being a pale lady with long auburn hair in loose-fitting clothing, in natural colours, very different from the contemporary fashion for restrictive corsets and structured, over-trimmed dresses. Gentlemen also adopted a less-structured look, with velvet jackets, soft shirts, flowing ties and longer hair. Morris & Co and Liberty's supplied goods which satisfied this demand, but these were only available for the well to do, as their hand-crafted nature meant they were out of reach of the working classes.

This lifestyle is depicted in the *Punch* cartoon, 'The Six-Mark Tea-Pot' (Plate1), which depicts an aesthetically dressed bride and groom within an aesthetic setting – a new definition of human and domestic beauty within a framework where art and life were in unison. With time Japanese influences joined with these domestic ones, and aesthetes became recognizable through their use of extravagant dress, exaggerated poses, including limp-handedness

THE SIX-MARK TEA-POT.

Æsthetic Bridegroom. " IT IS QUITE CONSUMMATE, IS IT NOT ?"
Intense Bride. " IT IS, INDEED ! OH, ALGERNON, LET US LIVE UP TO IT ! "

1 'The Six-Mark Teapot': Punch *cartoon
from 1880*

and an exaggerated form of speech which included set pieces such as 'utterly utter', a diverse range of objects including floral wallpapers, sunflowers and blue china.

All this occurred within a society that was undergoing rapid urbanization and industrialization; and aestheticism is, at least in part, a reaction against these changes. As the pre-existing order was destroyed, so its values were challenged, such that by 1870 a polarity had developed between the aesthetes who wanted to 'elevate taste into a scientific system', and those they termed the "Philistines" who were rejected because they were unable 'to see the true and the beautiful'.[2]

Those who were wealthy enough to afford new fashionable houses on high ground on the outskirts of the expanding towns, somewhere they could escape the worst of the crowded conditions, smoke and smells, but with easy access to both countryside and town centre, were well placed to adopt aesthetic principles. As designs of terracotta panels became available from the leading brick manufacturers the insertion of a sunflower panel (or two) in a prominent position could externally signal adherence to the movement, while the family could live out its other manifestations inside their private retreat from reality, with the woman of the house becoming the guardian of the dream.

The housing which was erected on the eastern side of Salisbury – in the Milford area – around the end of the 1800s is typical of this trend for the well-to-do to move away from the city centre. In the 30 years after 1871 the city expanded outside its traditional boundaries both to the east and to the west, in the latter case setting in motion a trend which continues inexorably to this day. Growth to the north concentrated initially on land within the boundaries, between Castle Street and the London Road, and that to the south was in general a somewhat later process.

2 Bedford Park, Turnham Green. Developed by Jonathan Carr, following his purchase of the land in 1876, architect Richard Norman Shaw. This was an aesthetic retreat on the outskirts of London which allowed the rising middle classes with cash to spare to combine a form of 'dream world' living, with a daily commute to a career in the City, thanks to the newly developed tube line. Shown here is 17 Blenheim Road, a typical example of the houses constructed.

Although no specific information survives as to whether Salisbury families living in houses decorated with sunflowers embraced aestheticism, examination of census records allows a consideration as to whether or not they fitted the typical profile of those who did. Developments along the Wilton Road, or up the Devizes Road, did sometimes incorporate decorative elements, but these were generally fairly minimal, and standardised. For more imaginative embellishments we need to look east, to the Milford area, where sunflowers are displayed in some quantity. The premise that a high sunflower count indicates a high concentration of aesthetic devotees leads us to the area around Manor Road with Bourne Avenue to the north and Fowlers Road to the south.

Number 20 Manor Road was also known as Manor House, though it was clearly the road that gave its name to the house, rather than the other way round. The road appears, with its present name, on the 1881 Ordnance Survey map, but there are no buildings on it. The house has a great deal of red terracotta decoration, especially to the two gables, and to the head of the central bay below (Plate 3), which is where the sunflowers can be found.[3] Even the front boundary wall has terracotta inserts, with leafy decoration among them (Plate 4).

3 Sunflowers (left) and 4 Terracotta decoration in boundary wall (above), both 20 Manor Road

In the census of 1901, the first to show people living in Manor Road, the household at Number 20 consisted of a 68 year old solicitor, George Nodder, and his wife and sister-in-law, together with two servants. [4] The aesthetic movement seems to have appealed to women as much as, and quite possibly more than, men, and it may be reasonable to suspect that it was the wife and sister-in-law, Caroline and Mary, who were responsible for either choosing a house with this kind of decoration, or indeed specifying it, if in fact the house was built for the family. In the absence of direct evidence it is of course possible that the sunflowers were simply the choice of a speculative builder who considered them a fashionable addition but was ignorant of the meaning behind them!

5 Non-terracotta, Hillcote, Manor Road   6 Sunflower panels, 31 Fowlers Road

Separated from Number 20 these days by a block of flats, though on the 1901 Ordnance Survey map they appear to be next door neighbours, is the road's most distinguished house, Hillcote. A masterwork of Salisbury's leading late 19th century and early 20th century architect, Fred Bath. Hillcote has a profusion of decorative embellishments (Plate 5), but among them is nothing that can be identified as a sunflower. It is known to have been built for its 1901 occupier, Ambrose Tucker, who was a bank manager. That serious profession might seem slightly at odds with an allegiance to something as flighty as the aesthetic movement, and the Hillcote decoration, where it can be traced to historic precedents, is classical in flavour. However the verve, zip and energy of the house does not totally accord with the traditional perception of bank managers, and too much should perhaps not be read into the absence of sunflowers.

To the south, 31 Fowlers Road, also known in some periods as Hill Brow, has some very prominent terracotta panels, Fisherton Grey brick in colour rather than red, and clearly containing sunflowers (Plate 6). Another panel shows the date of 1883, and it seems probable that the house was built for William Cripps, who in 1891 occupied it with his sister Sarah and brother Francis, plus one servant.[5] William had established a very successful grocery business on the corner of Catherine Street and Milford Street, and in 1881 was living there, above the shop. The story of growing financial prosperity and a move to the eastern suburbs must have been a fairly common one, together with less stress and more time to indulge in new fashions such as the aesthetic movement. Again, it may have been the sister who was the prime mover in attaching sunflowers to the new house. The grocery premises at 1 Catherine Street are now occupied by Specsavers, but lettering referring to the former Cripps business can still just be made out on the Milford Street frontage.

While terracotta was the chief medium for

7 Door-head at Chulmleigh, Elm Grove Road

displaying the sunflower symbol, there are a few instances of the use of other materials, of which the most striking may be the door-head to what is now 7 Elm Grove Road, between Manor Road and Fowlers Road (Plate 7). A date-stone on the house shows its construction in 1896, and also has the initials of Hubert Ware, for whom it was built. The Ware family were prominent in the local leather trade, with a base at 4 Endless Street, where their business sign is believed to survive behind later coverings. In 1901 Hubert's father, Edward, was still living in what had been the family home since at least 1871, 2 Somerset Villas, also in Elm Grove Road.[6] In fact the census appears to show this as only three doors away from Number 7, but all the houses now visible in the road look post-1871 in date. In 1901 the households of both Edward and Hubert included two servants, which seems fairly typical of the more prosperous families that inevitably a search for sunflowers leads us to. In the case of Hubert one of the servants, Agnes Andrews, is classed as a 'nurse', a profession immediately explained by the three preceding entries in the census. These were children, aged five, four and three. Their mother Sarah provided the name for the house, which when first built was called Chulmleigh, her birthplace in Devon. The family's story can be traced from the house's construction to the present day, since the current owner and occupier is Hubert Ware's daughter-in-law. The step of only one generation across 114 years must be fairly unusual.

The door-head to Chulmleigh is a remarkable artefact, following no obvious precedents and showing the inventiveness and self-confidence that is typical of the period, and more particularly typical of Fred Bath. However,

8 Petros Villas, Devizes Road (above), and 9 Date & flower panel, Petros Villas (right)

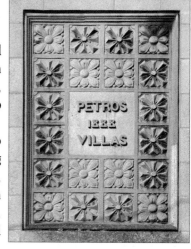

the rest of the exterior is quite restrained, and there is no known evidence that links him with the building. The sunflowers here are of stone, contained in the volutes in the centre of the top element to the door-head.

The sunflowers of Milford seem to corroborate the link to the aesthetes, revealing families in the upper strata of the middle classes, comfortably off and with time, particularly in the case of the women, to take an interest in, and declare an allegiance to, a relatively rarefied trend in current thinking. However sunflowers, or at least emblems that can be reasonably interpreted as referring to them, are not entirely absent in the new housing of the slightly less prosperous classes, westwards from the old city.

Petros Villas, a group of four houses on the south side of the Devizes Road (Plate 8), can be seen as perhaps a weak reflection of the tendencies being celebrated a mile to the east. It was built in 1888, as demonstrated on a plaque in the centre of its front elevation – and the rest of the plaque is made up of flowers (Plate 9). The plaque is of cast cement, which might just be seen as a cheap substitute for natural stone, except that the houses themselves are actually built of concrete blocks, like some others of similar date in the lower Devizes Road area.

The plaque material may in fact have been seen as a demonstration of modernity, but its flowery motifs are clearly partly at least aesthetic in origin. The stories of those living in Petros Villas bear out this impression of a rather-watered down echo of goings-on further east. In 1891 the head of household at 1 Petros Villas was John Batchelor, a 'building surveyor and clerk of works', quite conceivably the person who had overseen construction of the houses three years earlier. With his wife Emma he had six children, not by the standards of the day too tight a squeeze into the four bedrooms that the house probably possessed.[7] In 1881 they had been living at 25 Clifton Terrace, which the Ordnance Survey map published that year shows to be what is now Clifton Road, a hundred yards from Petros Villas, though its houses give the appearance of being later in date. This may largely be the effect of the ruthless stripping-away of original doors and windows that so many of Salisbury's terrace houses have been subject to in the last two decades.

By the 1901 census 1 Petros Villas was the home of four sisters with the surname Parham, aged from 33 to 44, all single and all 'living on own means'. Their income source becomes clear from the census of ten years earlier, which shows them living in Torquay with their father and mother, the latter a wine merchant who was born in Broad Chalke. A devotion to the aesthetic movement would not have been unlikely for such a quartet, even if they were perhaps living in reduced circumstances, and the movement's symbol on their house was not of the classiest kind.

Numbers 2 and 3 Petros Villas were homes in 1891 to a railway guard and a commercial traveller respectively, and their families, and in both cases one servant, a fact which might be of surprise to those in equivalent occupations today but was commonplace in the 19th century. The final house, 4 Petros Villas, was occupied in 1891 by a widow, Ann Brock, and her two daughters, aged 26 and 39, and again single. The latter are shown as dressmakers, though in the previous two censuses family members are generally described as 'harness makers'.[8] There were also two boarders, both single women, one a cook, and one, called Eva Aynsley, aged 41 and born in Paddington, described as a 'poetess'. Some unfathomable story lies within that one noun – did she make a living as a poet, which seems unlikely, or was she, in fact, 'living on own means', and dabbling in verse as a way of passing the time? Such a person would have been eminently eligible to belong to the aesthetic movement.

Interestingly the cult of the sunflower was not exclusively a domestic matter in Salisbury. Pinckney's Bank (on the corner of Winchester Street and Queen Street) was built in an Old English style in 1878. It has a very prominent sunflower panel on the Winchester Street façade and others on the roof (Plate 10).

At much the same time the Wilts & Dorset Bank was built in a classical style (1869 and extended twice) on Blue Boar Row at the northern side of the Market Square. Faced with the choice of investing in a bank that expressed its values in classicism or another that proclaimed its aesthetic ideals it seems that the people of Salisbury may have preferred the classical – by 1898 Pinckney's had amalgamated with the Wilts & Dorset. Both buildings still survive. The Wilts & Dorset has become LloydsTSB, while the Queen Street premises, now known as Cross Keys House, has mixed business uses.

Much work remains to be done on the extent of the aesthetic movement in Salisbury. For example was there a Rational Dress society in the city? Sarum Chronicle would be glad to

10 Terracotta panel on Cross Keys House, Winchester Street elevation

receive information from anyone with firm evidence that family members embraced aestheticism. While the sunflowers may remain, it is unlikely that those who today inhabit the houses which bear them are aware of their association with the aesthetic movement, and thus any message they were intended to convey has been nullified by the passage of time.

References/Notes

Background:

E Aslin *The Aesthetic Movement: prelude to Art Nouveau*, London, 1969, especially Chapter 2: 'Red Brick and Sunflowers'.

W Hamilton, *The Aesthetic Movement in England*, New York & London 1986

Herbert Norris & Oswald Curtis, *Costume & Fashion Volume Six: The Nineteenth Century*, London & Toronto, 1933

1   Oscar Wilde, *The Critic as Artist*, 1891
2   Hamilton, vii
3   Botanical accuracy was not always to the fore when terracotta was being designed, and 'sunflowers' sometimes have to be more loosely defined as any flower shown on a building.
4   1901 census Manor Rd, RG13/1952, folios 153-5
5   1891 census Fowler's Rd, RG12/1618 folio 30
6   1901 census Elm Grove Rd, RG13/1952, folios 156-7
7   1891 census 1-4 Petros Villas, Devizes Rd, RG12/1617, folio 60
8   1901 census 1-4 Petros Villas, Devizes Rd, RG13/1952, folio 53

Francis Topp, Father and Son: the Fortunes and Misfortunes of a Coombe Bissett Family

Jennifer Acornley

Francis Topp (senior) was born, almost literally, with a silver spoon in his mouth. His maternal grandfather William Kirley made his will on the 13 July 1583 and bequeathed to the 'childe wherewith my daughter Toppe nowe goeth if it shalbe born alive two silver spoons'. The child was born alive and was christened Francis at Berwick St John on 31 August 1583. Through the long life ahead he shared with contemporaries of his rank the dangers and dilemmas of a nation at war with itself, and the penalties of backing the wrong side. He fathered sons, one of whom, also Francis, enriched by trade, befriended an impoverished duke and unconventional duchess, and died a baronet mired in scandal. The careers of father and son took them around England and the continent, but their lives were rooted in the family estate at Coombe Bissett, three miles south-west of Salisbury.

Francis was the eldest child of Robert and Alice Topp (née Kirley) of Bridmore, Berwick St John. The family had leased the farm from the Uvedale family for three generations, at least from 1547 and Edmund Topp of the Stockton branch of the family was there in 1647. The family was involved in many disputes over the rights of the Lord of Cranborne Chase over the lands at Bridmore as the Topps made fences and ditches to keep out the deer, saying that they were outside the bounds of the Chase.

It was through William Kirley, described as a yeoman, that the Topps came to hold land in Coombe Bissett, as he bequeathed all his 'landes tenements and heriditaments' there to his daughter Alice. He had held this land since at least 1560, but in the herald's visitation of Wiltshire in 1623 he is described as of Wilton, where he can also be found in 1576 assessed to pay £1 13s 4d for a graduated tax based on land ownership and goods – the highest assessment on the Wilton list. In his will he left 3s 4d to St. Mary's church in Wilton, but asked to be buried by his pew in Coombe Bissett.

From 1241 Coombe Bissett had been divided into two manors, one of which became the property of Winchester College in 1385, and the other was

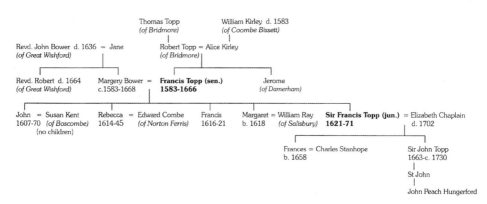

Topp family pedigree

held by a succession of indirect descendants of the Bissett family and others, until it became part of the Radnor estate in 1777. The first surviving record of Robert and Francis Topp in Coombe Bissett is in 1608-9 in an account book from Winchester College. Later documents show that at Michaelmas 1639 Francis Topp, gent, was paying a shilling quit rent to the College manor to excuse him from manorial services, and in 1652 a shilling quit rent to the other manor.

On 15 May 1606 Francis married Margery Bower at Sturminster Marshall in Dorset. They were both aged 23, and she was the daughter of John Bower, rector of Great Wishford, and his wife Jane. A year later their eldest son, John, was born and baptised in Great Wishford. Four more children followed, Rebecca (1614) Francis (1616, died April 1621), Margaret (1618) and Francis (September 1621), all baptised in Coombe Bissett.

Francis became involved in local affairs, witnessing wills and drawing up inventories. Among these was the will of William Barber alias Waylett, who was the collector of rents for the Winchester College manor. He died in 1616 and his assets were valued at £170 14s 2d. A much more modest estate of £25 10s, but possibly a more personal one, was that of John Lipps, a tailor in Coombe Bissett, who died in 1628. He made his 'loving friend' Francis Topp the overseer of his will and left him 12d for his pains. Francis was also present at *inquisitions post mortem* held between 1630 and 1633 in Salisbury, West Harnham, Wishford and Westbury.

Francis's father-in law, John Bower, died in 1636. His will, made ten years earlier, assigned the advowson of Wishford jointly to his cousin William Bower and Francis Topp. His son, Robert, became the next rector of Wishford. Robert Bower and Francis were the overseers of the will, and the very considerable estate was valued at £2,211 7s 6d.

An official duty undertaken by Francis in May 1641 was an appointment as the 'High Collector' of a lay subsidy (a form of taxation) in the hundreds of

Branch and Dole, Cawden and Cadworth, Downton, Chalke, Underditch and Frustfield. Of the twelve residents in Coombe Bissett eligible for the tax, Francis paid the highest amount of £1 12s.

By 1641 the Topps' three eldest children were married, all to members of established local families. John married Susan Kent from Boscombe, Rebecca, Edward Combe from Norton Ferris (near Mere, but then in Somerset), and Margaret, William Ray from Salisbury. Rebecca died in March 1644/5, three years after her marriage, and was buried at Kilmington, where there is a touching memorial to her in the church.

National events were now to take over as the rift between parliament and the king deepened, and by the summer of 1642, the civil war had begun. The Topps seem to have had royalist sympathies, although at the beginning of the war Wessex was mainly for parliament. Fighting occurred in Salisbury between 1643 and 1645 with each side holding the city for short periods, and the royalist commander Lord George Goring was based there for five weeks in December and January 1644-5. His notoriously ill-disciplined troops committed 'horrible outrages and barbarities' in the countryside. The presence of at least one of his men in Coombe Bissett is recorded by an entry in the church burial register as 'Solomon, a souldier under Lord Goringes comand buried Jan. 3rd 1644/5'. Salisbury was re-taken by parliament in the spring.

The royalist forces were based at Longford Castle until it was surrendered to Cromwell in October 1645, and the parliamentarian garrison was at Faulston House in Bishopstone from1645. It was here that the Faulston House Committee met to raise money and deal with 'delinquents'. An entry in the Faulston Day Book records that Francis Topp went to Faulston on 16 May 1645 to pay £5 'upon the propositions', which were levies on personal property. They were officially loans which were to be repaid with 8% interest, but never were. He also lent £5 to Captain d'Oyley, an early commander of the garrison. (A will inventory of 1641 valued forty sheep at £10.)

The early months of 1645 had seen the rise of a group called the clubmen. They were men tired of the demands of soldiers for food and quarter and of being plundered by both sides. There were said to be 700 members in Salisbury, and Mr Edward Topp from Stockton was named as one of their leaders. On 5 August the Parliamentarian leader, Sir Thomas Fairfax, was confronted by 10,000 clubmen on Hambledon Hill in Dorset. Cromwell persuaded some of them to go home, but some opened fire, and Cromwell and his Model Army counter-attacked resulting in 12 clubmen being killed and 400 imprisoned in Iwerne Courtney church. Some of the leaders, 'country gentlemen and ministers', were taken to Sherborne. This was the end of the clubmen's resistance.

It is probable that John Topp was one of the clubmen. On 20 August 1645, two weeks after the events on Hambledon Hill, John Topp of 'Combe,

Gent.', was brought before the Faulston House Committee and paid £10 for his 'enlargement' or release from imprisonment, which suggests he was fighting there. On 11 September the vicar of Coombe Bissett, Henry Beach, was also brought before the Committee, as he 'had combined with the clubmen and had been heard to say that as the parliament had abused their power, it was now time to take the staff out of their hands and walk with it'. He was also to pay £10. At the end of December John Topp was once again at Faulston on 'suspicion of delinquency'. He promised a horse worth £5 and £30 in money. His father was called there 'a second time' to subscribe £10 for his 'twenty-fifth part'. This was a levy on personal property over £200, and Francis Topp's younger brother, Jerome Topp of Damerham, was also called to pay £10 either on the Propositions or for his twenty-fifth part.

In January 1649 King Charles was executed and the Commonwealth established. A documented change brought about by the new order was that Henry Beach was removed from his vicarage and replaced by Mr Hector Carpenter, minister. Francis Topp's brother-in-law, Robert Bower, was also ejected from Great Wishford and replaced by a 'conforming' minister.

There is no record of the Topps' younger son, Francis, during this period until October 1656 when he was issued with a passport to Brabant in the Spanish Netherlands by the King of Spain. Now 35, it is probable that he had been a merchant for some years, which he certainly was two years later when he was in Antwerp. This career may have been influenced by the Topps of Stockton who were clothiers. It was in Antwerp that he began his association with William Cavendish, Marquis of Newcastle, who was living impoverished in exile there, having left England after the Battle of Marston Moor with only £90. The marquis and his wife Margaret had been in Antwerp since 1648, renting the house of the painter Rubens from his heirs, and Francis was able to help them with funds. Lady Cavendish had a maid, Elizabeth Chaplain, who had come from England with her, and who was her trusted companion. Elizabeth had pawned trinkets to raise money and had been sent back to England to obtain funds from Lady Cavendish's brother. By 1658 Francis Topp and Elizabeth Chaplain were married and their daughter, Frances, was born. The marquis continued to require considerable financial assistance, and after the restoration in 1660 the Topps returned to his estate at Welbeck in Nottinghamshire where Francis managed his affairs.

Several letters written by Francis junior have survived from this period. One shows that he may still have had trading connections, as he wrote to the marquis from Bristol in November 1661 saying, 'I send some wine, tobacco and other commodities, the best that can be had. I shall soon have some excellent tobacco, as many ships are expected daily from Spain.' Another letter, sent from Bath in August 1663 to Andrew Clayton the marquis's steward, has a postscript written by Henry Beach, who had been restored as vicar of Coombe

Bissett. It appears that Beach had purchased the right to the tithes of the parish of Slingsby in Yorkshire and was having difficulty in receiving the payments. Francis signs himself, as he did in other letters, 'your affectionate friend' to Mr. Clayton, which is interesting in the light of future events. At about this time the marquis conveyed his manor of Tormarton, Gloucestershire to Francis.

An infant son of Francis and Elizabeth died in March 1661 and was buried in Coombe Bissett. A second son, John, was born in 1663. As Francis's brother and sister-in-law John and Susan Topp were childless a deed of covenant to levy a fine was drawn up in January 1665 to pass the Coombe Bissett property to him, Francis paying £300 to John, who would also receive £55 annually. This document describes their house that John and Susan were to 'occupy, possess and enjoy' as all the east part of the 'Mansion or dwelling house . . . served with the Entry, with all the rooms above and below, belonging thereunto, and also one halfe of the Gardens and Orchards belonging to the same'.

Francis Topp senior died in January 1666 at the age of 83. His will has not survived but his probate inventory shows that his house was comfortably furnished. There were covered chairs and cushions, 26 pictures, plate, a brass clock and books valued at £20. Goods in a house at Wishford, one of two leasehold properties Margery Topp had inherited from her brother Robert who died in 1664, were worth £4 10s. There is no mention of crops or any livestock except a mare. The total value given was £789 11s. Margery Topp died in January 1668 and her son Francis became a baronet in July that year.

At Welbeck the marquis had been made a duke in 1664. His wife was an unusual and remarkable woman for her time and was notable for her unconventional dress and manners. She was a prolific writer of essays, novels and plays for publication, a philosopher and scientific theorist, and a kind of proto-feminist; in 1664 she dedicated her Sociable Letters to her 'Friend and former maid Mrs. Elizabeth Topp'. Both Francis and the duchess were unpopular with the duke's children from his first marriage and with the Welbeck servants, probably because they took too much notice of any financial extravagances, the duchess having taken over the management of the elderly duke's affairs after Francis left Welbeck in 1669. On 3 November 1670 the duke received an anonymous letter in which it was said that his honour had been much reduced by the duchess, and that she had committed adultery with Francis Topp. It was not until July 1671 that John Booth, one of the conspirators in the writing of the letter, made a full confession, and it became known that the steward, Andrew Clayton, had originated the allegation. This confession was too late for Sir Francis, as he died early in February 1671, less than a year after his brother John who had died in July 1670.

Sir Francis's will had been made in November 1668. By this time, as well as the land in Coombe Bissett and the manor of Tormarton, he had land in Acton Turville, Glos. and in Nottinghamshire, and leased a house in Aldgate,

London. He also held the lease of the two tenements in Great Wishford after the decease of his 'deare Mother'. He made arrangements for a marriage portion of £2,000 for his daughter Frances, and appointed John Willoughby of Bristol, merchant, to act as a trustee during his son John's minority. His dearly beloved wife was his executrix.

Lady Elizabeth Topp wrote her will in 1688. She passed her interest in land in Lincolnshire to her daughter Frances, the income from which should in 'noe wayes be intermedled with' by her husband Charles Stanhope. She also left Frances her 'Oglebey's Bible' and her biggest cabinet and 'all things therein'. Perhaps these included some of the 'toys' redeemed from the pawnbroker in Antwerp. When she died in 1702, she was taken to Coombe Bissett to be laid 'next to her late deare husband', as she had asked.

Susan Topp died in January 1695, 25 years after her husband John. Her probate inventory shows that they had carried on farming the Topps' land, as 'horses, wagon, dung pott, plows, harrows and harnesse' are listed, as well as corn, 240 sheep and 35 young lambs. After the death of Sir Francis's son Sir John in c.1730, the land passed from his daughter St John, to her son John Peach Hungerford.

A book of reference dated 1782 concerning land later held by Lord Radnor describes land held by J P Hungerford Esq in Coombe Bissett and also in Homington, where Thomas Feltham was the tenant. Near the 'House, Barns, Garden and Orchard' were 'Broad Mead' and most significantly, 'Land Mead against Cawdon Ditch'. Cawden Ditch, or Cawden Water is a small stream that joins the Ebble in Homington and was part of the ancient parish boundary between Coombe Bissett and Homington. This location suggests that these eight acres of the Topp's land were centred on Tottens Farm, the easternmost farm in the village in the 19th century. Perhaps its name is a corruption of Topp. Tottens Farmhouse was demolished in the 1990s for a housing development, but it is unlikely that that modest building was the one there in the 16th century. The book also lists 41 acres of arable land in the North Common Field, and approximately 8 acres of pasture. The 6 pieces of land in Homington were all on Cawden Down, now called Homington Down, and were on the Britford boundary. They had an area of approximately 65 acres and are shown on the Homington inclosure map of 1787. In 1789 the land was sold to T H Jervoise of Britford, and in 1800 became part of the Radnor estate. So ended 200 years of the Topp family in Coombe Bissett.

Notes

1 TNA PROB 11/66: will of William Kirleye, proved 1583
2 WSA 1764/22
3 Fry, E A (1902-04) 'A Calendar of feet of fines for Wiltshire' in *WNQ* vol 4 , 445; Marshall, G W (1882) *Visitation of Wiltshire 1623*, 57; Ramsay, G D (1954) *Two sixteenth century taxation lists, 1545 and 1576* (WRS vol 10), 144
4 Winchester College Muniments WCM

4779; WSA 490/770

5 WSA P5/1606/51 William Waylett alias Barber; WSA P5/11 Reg/11F: John Lipps

6 Fry, E A, and G S (1893) *Abstracts of Wiltshire IPMs: Charles I.* (Index Library 23), 101-3, 232

7 TNA E179/259/22

8 von Roemer, M. (1914-15) 'Notes on the descendants of Edward Combe, of Bridsor in Tisbury' *WNQ* vol. 8, 63-73 (on p 73)

9 Waylen, J (1891) 'The Falston Day Book' *WANHM* vol.26, 347

10 *J House of Commons* (1645) vol 4, 234, 484

11 Waylen, J (1891) 'The Falston Day-Book' *WANHM* vol 26, 350, 351, 359, 365

12 Bodington, E J (1917-19) 'The Church Survey of Wiltshire' *WANHM* vol. 40, 44

13 Nottingham Univ Lib PW2 X3: pass issued to Francis Topp

14 Cavendish, Margaret (ed E. Bridges) (1814) *A true relation of the Birth, Breeding and Life of Margaret Cavendish, Duchess of Newcastle, Written by Herself* Lee Priory Press; Jones, Kathleen (1988) *A Glorious Fame* London, Bloomsbury; Worsley, Lucy (2007) *Cavalier*. London: Faber

15 Hist. MSS. Com. Portland MSS II: letter to the Marquis of Newcastle; Nottingham Univ Lib, PW1 505: letter to Andrew Clayton

16 WSA 490/187

17 WSA P5/1666/33: Francis Topp

18 Oxford DNB online

19 TNA PROB11/351: will of Sir Francis Topp 1676

20 TNA PROB11/472: will of Lady Elizabeth Toppe or Topp, proved 1703

21 WSA P8/6: Susan Topp

22 WSA 490/1050; 490/187

Southampton's Brokage Books – their relevance to Salisbury

Winifred A Harwood

On Tuesday 1 February 1448 Stephen Kynge, carter, left Southampton with
one cart bound for Salisbury. On the cart were three barrels of herring and 126
gallons of wine for John Macyn. Kynge paid 10d in tolls of which, five pence was
for local custom, four pence for brokage and one penny for pontage.[1]

This is typical of the numerous entries which can be found in the Southampton
brokage books. The books are highly acclaimed as the best surviving
source for England's inland trade, for which documentation is relatively rare.
They reveal how goods which had arrived in Southampton by sea were then
distributed by cart or packhorse to towns and villages, markets and fairs,
ecclesiastical and cloth-producing centres across many parts of England. Carts
left Southampton laden with goods for nearby places in Hampshire, as well
as more distant destinations, such as Bristol, Coventry, Gloucester, London,
Oxford and Salisbury.

On Tuesday 1 February 1448, a total of 21 carts left Southampton through
the Bargate. Of these, two went to each of the following places:- Andover,
London, Romsey and Winchester, while 13 went to Salisbury. These 13 carts
took a total of 378 gallons and one galley barrel of wine for John Hancok, John
Macyn and Thomas Whytynge; 70 barrels of herring for Richard Bele, John
Dawbeney, John Halle, and John Macyn; 48 salmon for John Macyn; and, for
John Halle, one bale of gall, the dye which was used in ink making, dyeing and
medicinal purposes. The entries for this one day in February demonstrate the
strong trading connection which existed between Salisbury and Southampton
in this period and highlight the relevance of the brokage books to the history of
Salisbury.

That there are such detailed accounts of what happened is due to the
payment of tolls at Southampton's Bargate. As carts entered or left the town
a town official, known as the Bargate broker, collected and recorded the three
tolls of brokage,[2] local custom[3] and pontage.[4] As he did so he also recorded
the number of carts and the names of the carters, the goods and quantities they
carried, the person for whom the commodities were being transported and the

towns towards which the carts were heading. Although numerous carts entered the town laden with cloth and wool and with a variety of other commodities including corn, lime, malt and skins, it was the flow of commodities leaving the town which helped generate a source of great value, the Southampton brokage books. They are a unique set of accounts the likes of which exist for no other town in England.

The surviving brokage books, held by the Southampton Archives Services, cover a period from c.1430 to 1566 but are particularly useful for those years of the 15th century when the Italians were trading through the port.[5] Attention was drawn to the value of this useful source when, between 1941 and 1993, five books were edited and published by the Southampton Record Society and Southampton Records Series. The books are mostly written in Latin and in a 15th century hand and require transcribing and translating before information can be used.[6] While the printed volumes obviously have the advantage of being translated and include indexes which assist in the search for people and most places and commodities these do not accommodate total entries for major centres, or common commodities such as wine, woad and herring. Analysis of books in this form is both time-consuming and laborious.

A few years ago The Overland Trade Project was set up at the University of Winchester. One of its aims was to enter the information from the brokage books on to a database.[7] While remaining faithful to the original document, data had to be capable of being sorted, counted and analysed. Therefore, place names, spelling of commodities and measurements have been standardized.[8] Original surnames have been retained but also entered in a standardized form for counting purposes. Place names are grid referenced, as the database is also linked to a mapping system which enables results to be displayed in map form.[9] The work is ongoing but the value and scope of the database is already apparent, enabling not only the commodities of trade, but also the people and places linked through trade, to be closely examined. The findings discussed here are drawn from the records of the nine years already entered on the database.[10]

It is already recognized that the two most important towns with which Southampton was linked commercially in this period were London and Salisbury. Salisbury is the town with which this article is primarily concerned, and two commodities, wine and woad have been selected for close study. For much of the 15th century, Southampton was a busy international port. Numerous local vessels occupied in England's coastal trade, and carracks, galleys and ships engaged in trade overseas, entered and left the port. Ships arrived with cargoes of slates from Devon, tin and fish from Cornwall, and linen and canvas via the Channel Islands, pitch and bow-staves from the Baltic and wax from Portugal.[11] The port also flourished as fleets of carracks and galleys arrived from Florence, Genoa and Venice.

The Italian fleets brought with them silk, spices, wine and other exotic luxury goods, as well as vital mordants and dyes for the cloth industry. Having unloaded their cargoes in Southampton, the carracks sailed on to the Low Countries where they filled their holds with commodities typical of the northern regions, felt hats, linen and skins from the Baltic. These were brought ashore in Southampton where huge consignments of cloth and wool from the Cotswolds, Dorset, Hampshire and Wiltshire, tin from the West Country, and pewter, were loaded into the Italian holds for the homeward voyage.[12] Brokage book entries for Wednesday 17 October 1492 show as many as 24 carts arriving in Southampton laden with wool that day.[13] The success of Southampton in this period depended on this exchange of commodities. Wool and cloth were carried into the town by cart for dispatch overseas, and luxury goods, mainly for the London market, and raw products for the wool and cloth centres, arrived by sea for onward distribution to towns and villages across Hampshire, Wiltshire and beyond.

The Wiltshire town of Salisbury was an extremely important redistribution centre and marketing town in the 15th century. It was possibly England's leading cloth manufacturing centre, renowned for its fine striped 'ray cloth'.[14] By the late 14th century, Salisbury had already established a strong commercial relationship with London, as Salisbury rays were sent to the capital,[15] and it was also linked through trade with Southampton, a relationship which was flourishing in the 15th century. The importance of the Salisbury/Southampton connection is demonstrated by the entry in the Southampton Oak Book which shows that specially reduced rates of local custom had been agreed in 1329 for Salisbury burgesses, just as they had been agreed for places such as Bristol and London.[16] Complete exemption would have led to a considerable loss of income for Southampton due to the high volume of trade which left the port bound for Salisbury.

Local custom was generally collected with the other two tolls of brokage and pontage at the Bargate; however, it could also be collected at sea by the water bailiff and when this occurred the Bargate broker noted 'per mare' in his records. Thus when William Hayward passed through the Bargate on Saturday 1 February 1539, the broker collected four pence brokage and a penny pontage, but noted that custom had been paid 'by the sea'. Formalities recorded, Hayward set off towards Salisbury carrying a great bell on his cart for Roger Ellys.[17] An entry for Saturday 17 January 1540, however, shows that such transactions did not always proceed so smoothly; for when John Lovell passed through the Bargate, on his way to Salisbury with three hogshead of herring (nine barrels), for John Bekynghame, the broker noted that Lovell 'wold not feche hys bylle wherefore made hyme paye the hole custome 12d' in addition to the brokage of three pence and pontage of one penny.[18]

Wool and cloth from its hinterland were collected in Salisbury, from where it was taken to Southampton and, in return, raw products, dyes and mordants were taken to Salisbury, some for use or sale locally, and some for redistribution to cloth centres elsewhere. For example on Friday 20 October 1447-48, Ingram Twynham entered Southampton with a cart of cloth and left the town for Salisbury carrying nine baletts of woad for Thomas Pakkere.[19]

Salisbury merchants dominated the regional trade and London and Italian merchants generally dominated the luxury trade of Southampton, much of which went to the capital. The chart for 1447-48 clearly shows the important role Southampton played as an outport for London, and also that the role played by Salisbury as a regional redistribution centre was even more impressive. In that year out of a total of 2251 carts which left the town, 445 carts, 20% of the total, went to London, while as many as 784 carts (35%) went to Salisbury.

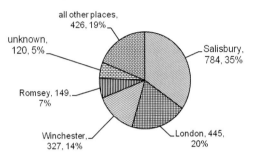

Figure 1: Cart destinations 1447-48

By 1492-93 the number of carts leaving Southampton had reduced to 1753. Those going to Salisbury had fallen back to 390 (22%) while a greater number of carts, 655, (37%) went to London. By 1539-40 the situation had changed again. Out of a total of 1308 carts, the greatest number going to a single place went to Salisbury, while the number travelling to London had declined greatly with only 46 (3%) going to the capital, less than one a week.

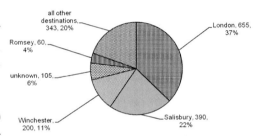

Figure 2: Cart destinations 1492-3

This scenario probably reflects changes in shipping patterns. As ship design developed and as navigation of the Thames improved, so more

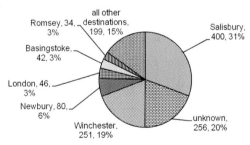

Figure 3: Cart destinations 1539-40

ships sailed directly to the port of London. The capital increasingly dominated overseas trade and lessened the need to use Southampton as an 'outport'. While the number of carts going to London declined, more carts than previously went to other more local towns, such as Newbury and Basingstoke, 80 and 42 respectively. The number going to Romsey had virtually halved to 34 compared with 60 in 1492-93, and considerably fewer when compared with the 149 in 1447-48.

The carts travelling to Salisbury carried a wide variety of commodities; feather beds,[20] felt and straw hats,[21] tennis balls,[22] various items of haberdashery, as well as useful and heavy commodities, iron, millstones, resin, tar and wax; and goods for consumption in terms of food and drink, fruit, vegetables and spices.[23] Fish, fresh, salted and smoked also went to Salisbury. In 1439-40 and 1447-48 large quantities were taken there for Richard Bele and included hake, red and white herring,[24] millwell and ling, and salt fish. Other Salisbury men who received large supplies of fish from Southampton included William Boket and Richard Cherite. Merchants, such as John Bewforde of London, sent herring and salmon to Salisbury in 1447-48; [25] and merchants Thomas Kneeswroth and John Smyth the London fishmonger, in 1477-78.[26]

Large quantities of wine left the port for destinations such as Salisbury, London and Winchester and Salisbury also received hops for brewing. (Fig 4) While London received an impressive amount of wine in 1492-93, almost 120,000 gallons (a figure which may have been closely followed the following year if only records had been complete) Salisbury, nevertheless, received over 34,000 gallons that year.

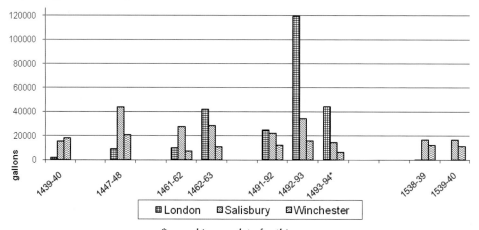

record incomplete for this year
Figure 4: Distribution of wine from Southampton

Wine was carried to Salisbury for merchants such as John Paynter, 1439-40;[27] John Hall in the mid 15th century;[28] Richard Cherite (1447-48 and 1491-92),[29] John Kelpryn (1477-8)[30] and Thomas Coke in the 1490s.[31] The brokage books of the early 1490s show large quantities of wine being sent to Thomas Coke and Richard Bartelmew. Indeed it took 15 carts to carry the 15 butts (1890 gallons) of wine to Salisbury for Bartelmew on Wednesday 8 May, 1492-93.[32] Various people and households also received wine from Southampton, such as the canons of the Close, M Chaunter in 1461-62, M Crowton in 1462-63 and Hugo Pavey in 1477-78; women such as My Lady of Hungerford in 1461-62, Scolastica Boket in 1491-92, and, in the same year, Isabel Ayleward.[33] On Saturday 25 May 1493, three carts carried 630 gallons of wine to Alice Gilpryn.[34] The inns of Salisbury were also supplied, The George in 1447-48,[35] The Greyhound in 1493-94,[36] The Angel in 1538-39.[37]

Wine also went to Salisbury for redistribution elsewhere, for example on five separate occasions in 1439-40 for John Dawy, a merchant of Wales. It was also redistributed to Moses Conteryne and Nicholas Longe of Bristol,[38] and to John Estfield, merchant of Bristol, who, in November 1492, had as much as 4410 gallons taken there for him. It took 23 carts to transport the 17 dolia and 1 butt of wine to Salisbury on behalf of this Bristol merchant.[39]

Analysing the commodities it becomes obvious that many of the Salisbury merchants, rather than specializing in a single product, dealt in a range of commodities. John Halle, the renowned and wealthy citizen and merchant of Salisbury, who died in 1479, was active for many years of the 15th century and features regularly in the brokage books. He is a useful example of a Salisbury merchant who received numerous goods from Southampton. As well as vital products for the cloth industry, alum, teasels and woad, he received various spices, fish, vegetables, hops, as well as canvas, hats, iron, tar and wax, to mention just a few. While some commodities may have been for his own use, others were certainly for sale, possibly from his shop which was called 'Doggehole' and which held a wide range of goods including wine.[40] To take just three examples of carters transporting goods for him:- on Tuesday 21 May, 1448, John Whyte, Thomas Smytht and William Hardynge carried three bundles containing 108 hats valued at 30 shillings, and 18 barrels of black soap. [41] On Saturday 31 August the same year Ingram Twynham and Thomas Hore left for Salisbury with 8 bales of madder and hops to the value of 23 shillings[42] and on Thursday 13 May 1462 John Gylberde carried one pipe of wine and one balett of woad .[43]

The brokage books help to identify other Salisbury merchants trading in a similar period to Halle, such as Thomas Pakker who had bowstaves, wine and woad carted for him,[44] William Lightfote, who traded in goods for the cloth industry, as well as in spices, herring, paper, scouring stones, wax and wine. [45] Men such as John Aporte, William Barlowe and William Swayne all benefited from their proximity to Southampton and, like Halle, dealt in a wide range of commodities.

The variety of goods taken to Salisbury was extensive, but undoubtedly, it was the raw products, vital to the cloth industry, which were amongst the most important cargoes to arrive in Southampton by sea. Carts left Southampton laden with bales of alum (a mordant used to fix dyes); with dyes, such as madder and woad; and with associated goods, such as canvas for making sarplars (bales of wool), cards for carding wool and teasels for raising the nap on cloth. The following entries are typical

on Monday 3 January 1463 Thomas Waryn left Southampton for Salisbury with 2 bales of madder and 8 skive (skevy or 5 cwt) teasels for William Boket[46] [and] on Saturday 28 April 1492 Roger White and William Waller carted 10 balett of woad and one case of soap to Salisbury for Richard Bartelmewe of Salisbury.[47]

Woad was an important dye and Salisbury's role in the distribution of this commodity is interesting. In financial year 1447-48 approximately 2927 baletts left Southampton of which 841 baletts (29%) went to Salisbury and 800 baletts (27%) to London; 314 baletts (11%) went to Winchester; 219 baletts (7%) went as far afield as Coventry (approximately 120 miles) which was well-known for its blue-dyed cloth in this period. A further 103 baletts were sent to Gloucester. Numerous small towns such as Bradford on Avon, Burford, Cirencester, Crewkerne, Exeter, Shaftesbury, Newbury, Oxford, Reading and Ringwood received less than 50 baletts.

However, not all of the woad which was taken to Salisbury, and attributed to Salisbury remained there; some was for onward distribution to other towns. For instance, between 8 and 15 November 1447, 60 baletts of woad were sent to Salisbury for John Clerk of Exeter[48] and between January and May 1448, 69 baletts went to Salisbury for Thomas and Robert Ede of Bruton.[49] Woad was

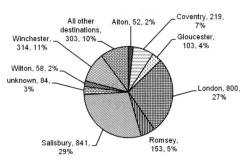

Figure 5: Distribution of woad from Southampton in 1447-8 (in baletts)

also sent to Salisbury for onward transmission to Bridgwater, Bristol, Frome, Glastonbury, Langport, Mells, Mere, Shepton Mallet, Warminster and Wodeland. Thus Salisbury is seen to be acting not only as a consumer of woad but also as a major redistributor to the West Country. By 1492-93 the total quantity of woad leaving the port by cart had fallen dramatically to just 169 baletts. An Act of 1489 had forbidden the import of Toulouse woad in foreign vessels.[50] In percentage terms, Salisbury was receiving more than anywhere else, but in terms of quantity, it was receiving far less woad from Southampton, when compared with the 841 baletts which went there in 1447-8. London which had accounted for 800 baletts in 1447-48 is not even shown on the chart (Fig 5), since, with only 13 baletts, it is included in the figures for 'all other destinations'.

By 1539-40 the distribution of woad had changed completely. The total quantity, 1077 baletts, was

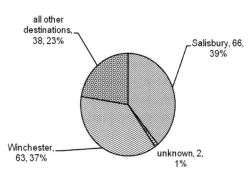

Figure 6: Distribution of woad from Southampton in 1492-93 (in baletts)

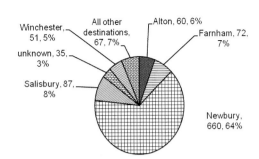

Figure 7: Distribution of woad from Southampton in 1539-40 (in baletts)

still far less than the 2850 baletts in 1447-48, and the places to which woad was taken had also changed. Only 8%, instead of 29% in 1447-48, went to Salisbury, and the greatest quantity, 660 baletts (64%) was sent to the Berkshire town of Newbury which had received only a negligible amount in 1447-48. That considerable quantities of woad were going to Newbury was perhaps not surprising since it was in this period that wealthy clothiers like John Winchcombe (c.1489-1557) were working in Newbury, producing kerseys and amassing great wealth.

Alum, like woad, was taken to Salisbury, both for use there and for redistribution elsewhere, to men such as Thomas and Robert Ede, merchants of Bruton.[51] The two bales of alum which were sent for John Blower of Taunton in October 1439 were taken there by John Hillere.[52] Hillere is only one of many carters whose journeys can be analysed with the help of the database. The Bere family is another example. At the beginning of this article it was seen that 21 carts left Southampton on Tuesday 1 February 1447-48, among the carters who travelled to Salisbury that day, were John Bere senior and junior. The Bere family carted there frequently, sometimes travelling alone, sometimes in a group of carters. It is not always possible to differentiate between Bere senior and junior. However, in 1447-48, between them, they travelled to Salisbury at least once a month as in October; the most cart/journeys to Salisbury, 15, were made in February, and the second greatest, 12, in January. They took ten carts there in July suggesting that travelling conditions did not prevent them from making the greatest number of journeys in the winter.

Carters, such as John Bere senior and junior, who travelled to Salisbury, and to numerous other places in England, were performing a valuable service when they distributed the goods which had arrived in Southampton by sea. Little did they realize that as they paid their tolls at Southampton's Bargate and as the Bargate broker recorded these tolls, they were also, albeit inadvertently, helping to create an extremely valuable and unique series of accounts. Now, 600 years later, modern technology is making the detail from the Southampton brokage books more easily searchable, and, ultimately, more accessible, to a much wider audience.

[Bibliography and notes overleaf]

Bibliography and Notes

Parts of this paper are included in the *Southampton Brokage Book, 1447-48*, edited by the author (SRS, 42, 2008) which has also been produced on CD, and on the Overland Trade Project Website at the University of Winchester. To find out more visit www.winchester. ac.uk and enter 'Overland Trade Project' in the search box. The interim results contain many useful maps.

SOUTHAMPTON ARCHIVES SERVICES
Southampton brokage books
SC5/5/3 1439-40
SC5/5/8 1447-48
SC5/5/13 1461-62
SC5/5/14 1462-63
SC5/5/22 1477-78
SC5/5/28 1491-92
SC5/5/29 1492-93
SC5/5/30 1493-94
SC5/5/37 1538-39
SC5/5/38 1539-40

Bettey, J H A *Regional History of England: Wessex from AD 1000*. London: Longman, 1986

Bunyard, B D M (ed) *Brokage Book of Southampton 1439-40*, (Southampton Record Society 40, 1941).

Cobb, H S (ed) *Port Book of Southampton 1439-40*, (SRS 5, 1961)

Coleman O (ed) *Brokage Book of Southampton 1443-44*, (2 vols, SRS 4, 1960)

Critall E, (ed) *Victoria History of the Counties of England: Wiltshire. 6:* London, 1962

Foster, B (ed) *Port Book of Southampton for 1435-36*, (SRS 7, 1963)

Harwood, W A (ed) *Brokage Book of Southampton, 1447-48*, (SRS 4, 2008)

Harwood, W A (ed) Brokage Book of Southampton, 1447-48 Wessex Historical Databases 1 [CD publication] (ISBN 0-9553778-0-3)

Harwood, W A 'The Customs System in Southampton in the Mid-Fifteenth Century' *Proceedings of the Hampshire Field Club and Archaeological Society*, vol 53, 1998

James, T B (ed) *Port Book of Southampton, 1509-10*, (2 vols SRS 32, 1990)

Platt, C *Medieval Southampton The Port and Trading Community, AD 1000-1600*. London: Routledge and Kegan Paul, 1973

Ruddock, A A *Italian Merchants and Shipping in Southampton 1270-1600* SRS 1 Southampton: Southampton University College, 1951

Stevens, K F and Olding, T E (eds) *Brokage Books of Southampton 1477-78 and 1527-28*, (SRS 28, 1985)

1 SC5/5/8, Tues 1 February 1448
2 Brokage was a toll levied originally for arranging the haulage of goods which varied with distance travelled
3 Local custom duty paid to broker on goods, though sometimes paid at sea to the water bailiff
4 Pontage a one penny toll levied on all vehicles entering or leaving the town through Bargate
5 Fewer Italian ships were seen in the Solent after *c*.1470 due a disruption in Anglo-Italian trading patterns
6 A few of the later books such as SC5.5.36 for 1537-38, are written in English
7 The Overland Trade Project is under the directorship of Professor M Hicks; Dr W A Harwood (the author) is responsible for designing, setting up and inputting data.
8 Wine, for instance, appears in the original text as barrels (32 gallons), hogsheads (63 gallons), pipes (126 gallons), butts (126 gallons) and dolia (252 gallons), but is entered on the database in gallons, with the original quantity retained in the notes.
9 Mapping is undertaken by Geodata of Southampton University, for examples see website
10 These years are 1439-40; 1447-48; 1461-63; 1491-94; 1538-40;

although brokage book 1477-78 is currently being entered onto the database and is sometimes referred to here, total figures for this year are not yet available.

11 Platt, 157-159; Foster, 13, 45, and 39; Cobb, 23 and 26.

12 Southampton became increasingly involved in the handling of tin from the West Country when a staple of metals was set up in 1492.

13 SC5.5.29 Wed 17 October 1492

14 Bettey, 116-117

15 VCH, *Wiltshire*, 6, 128

16 Harwood, [Customs System], 195

17 SC5.5.37 Sat 1 February 1539

18 SC5.5.38 Sat 16 January, 1540

19 SC5.5.8 Fri 20 October 1447

20 SC5.5.3 Four featherbeds were sent to Salisbury on Sat 19 March 1440

21 SC5.5.14 Sat 30 April 1463 when felt hats and straw hats were taken to Salisbury

22 SC5.5.28 Mon 25 June 1492

23 Spices:- a term which referred to dried fruits, sugar and rice as well as strongly flavoured spices

24 White herring, fresh or salted; red herring, salted and smoked

25 SC5.5.8 Thursday 17 February, 1448

26 SC5.5.22 Wed 18 February 1478 and Sat 21 February 1478

27 SC5.5.3 Wed 11 November 1439

28 See for example SC5.5.8 Fri 10 May 1448

29 See for example SC5.5.22 Sat 7 February 1478

30 SC5.5.22 Sat 8 November 1477

31 SC5.5.28 Thurs 13 September 1492

32 SC5.5.29 Wed 8 May 1493

33 SC5.5.13 and 28 13.61r6 and 28.39r5 and 13.41r9

34 SC5.5.29 Sat 25 May 1493

35 SC5.5.8 Fri 8 March 1448

36 SC5.5.30 Fri 17 May 1494

37 SC5.5.37 Wed 5 March 1539

38 SC5.5.8 Wed 28 August 1448

39 SC5.5.29 Wed 28 November 1492

40 *VCH, Wiltshire*, 6, 125.

41 SC5.5.8 Tues 21 May 1448

42 SC5.5.8 Sat 31 August 1448

43 SC5.5.13 Thurs 13 May 1462

44 See SC5.5.8 Fri 25 February 1448, Mon 15 January 1448, and Fri 20 October 1447 respectively;

45 For examples of commodities for wool and cloth industry see, SC5.5.8 Sat 20 January 1448, SC5.5.8 Fri 31 May 1448; for spices SC5.5.8 Wed 17 April 1448; for herring SC5.5.8 Sat 20 January 1448; for paper SC5.5.8 Sat 20 April 1448; scouring stones SC5.5.8 Thurs 17 February 1448; for wax SC5.5.8 Sat 20 January 1448; and for wine SC5.5.8 Mon 4 December 1447.

46 SC5.5.14 Mon 3 January 1463

47 SC5.5.28 Sat 28 April 1492

48 See for example SC5.5.8 Fri 10 November 1447

49 SC5.5.8 Mon 21 February 1448

50 Ruddock, 214

51 SC5.5.3 Wed 24 February 1440 and SC5.5.8 Mon 21 February 1448

52 SC5.5.3 Wed 27 October 1439

Celebrating 150 Years of Salisbury Museum

by Adrian Green

The First Museums

Salisbury Museum was founded at a time when new scientific discoveries were revolutionising our understanding of the natural world. The work of scientists such as Charles Darwin and Charles Lyell inspired a range of new subjects including archaeology and ethnography. Museums and public exhibitions were an important way for these new subjects to reach a wider audience.

Collecting antiquities, fossils and natural history specimens was a popular pastime amongst the educated middle classes. In Victorian Salisbury there were occasional exhibitions at the Guildhall. The owners of these collections shared a common concern that important archaeological discoveries were not staying in Salisbury, but were disappearing to the national museums in London.

The core of the Museum's collection is the 'Drainage Collection', a group of medieval finds from the open water channels or drains that used to run through the streets of Salisbury. These drains became a major health hazard and were replaced with underground sewers in the 1850s. During the construction work hundreds of everyday objects, lost over the centuries by local residents and visitors to Salisbury, were found. Rather than dispersing these finds to other institutions, such as the British Museum, a group of local gentlemen, led by Dr Richard Fowler, resolved to purchase the finds with the purpose of setting up a museum. The first meeting of the Museum Committee was held in July 1860 and the first public exhibition of what later become known as the 'Drainage Collection' took place in June 1861 in a room in the building adjoining the Market House. In 1864 the Museum moved to new premises in St Ann Street, which remained its home for more than a hundred years until the relocation to the King's House in 1981.

When Salisbury Museum was established it was the only one in the city, indeed one of fewer than a hundred museums open to the public in the whole of England. In 1867 it was joined by another, the Blackmore Museum, which opened in a separate building to its rear. This museum was built by William Blackmore, a wealthy solicitor and businessman from Salisbury, to house his collection of antiquities. Unlike the Salisbury Museum with its local focus, the Blackmore Museum was billed as a 'Stone Age Museum Illustrating the Prehistoric and Modern Savage'. Archaeological finds from across the world were displayed according to the recently established Palaeolithic (Old Stone Age) and Neolithic (New Stone Age) periods. It also housed ethnographic objects from world cultures

The Victorian interior of the Blackmore Museum

to illustrate how our distant ancestors lived. The most significant collection was the Squier and Davis collection of Native American archaeology, purchased by William Blackmore in New York in 1864.

In his address at the opening of the Blackmore Museum, William Blackmore stated that 'A . . . motive in the establishment of this Museum, has been the benefit of my native city, more particularly by giving increased means of study to the young men of Salisbury.' He also stated that it was established to 'increase knowledge' and was an institution where the visitor will be able to become 'acquainted with those relics of the Stone Age which tell us all we know of the earliest inhabitants of our own and other countries'.

The first honorary curators of the museums sought to bring the wider world to Salisbury. Therefore the geographical boundaries for collecting in both the Blackmore and the Salisbury and South Wiltshire Museums were not confined to Wiltshire. Natural history and ceramics were collected from across Britain, and when John Passmore Edwards became MP for Salisbury in 1880, Salisbury Museum accepted a gift from him of an Egyptian mummy and sarcophagus.

The Salisbury Museum and the Blackmore Museum were both managed by the same committee and had a joint honorary Director, Edward Thomas (E T) Stevens. As is the case today, the museums were independent, with financial support coming from subscribers and donations, in particular from William Blackmore himself.

Publication was an important activity for the museums. Salisbury and South Wiltshire Museum published its first extensive catalogue in 1864, the year that it opened at 42-44 St Ann Street. William Blackmore paid for the publication of the Blackmore Museum's first catalogue called *Flint Chips* in

1870. Both were written by E T Stevens. *Flint Chips* was both a scholarly publication and 'advertisement' for the Blackmore Museum. Since William Blackmore's business involved selling land for settlement and development in North America; *Flint Chips* would have been a useful way to demonstrate to his business contacts both his status, and his interest in North American archaeology.

William Blackmore had invested in land that was overvalued, and faced financial ruin, so he committed suicide in 1878. The first honorary Director, E T Stevens, also died in the same year.

There was no financial endowment for the Blackmore Museum, and as further supporters passed away the museums began to face financial problems. The museums, which had been amalgamated in 1878, became a charity in 1904 under the terms of the will of another key supporter, Mr W D Wilkes, but this did little to help with the day-to-day cash flow. A financial crisis in 1913 was only avoided because subscribers doubled their subscriptions and life members renewed their fees.

A Family Affair

Remarkably, the museums remained under the control of the same family for over ninety years. E T Stevens was William Blackmore's brother in law and when they both died William's brother, Dr Humphrey Blackmore, took over. He enrolled the support of his nephew, Frank Stevens, the youngest son of Edward Thomas Stevens, in 1913, who became the 'resident controller' and then Director after Dr Blackmore's death in 1929.

Frank Stevens was very keen to popularise the museums; he introduced a public lecture series, but a proposed Jubilee Festival in 1914 was cancelled due to the onset of war. In 1916 he published what was to become the first official guidebook to Stonehenge and after the war played a key role in co-ordinating the Salisbury Peace Pageant. Under Frank Stevens an important benefactor was William Wyndham of Orchard Wyndham in Somerset, who provided a specimen fund to help purchase museum objects, and met the costs of a series of extensions to the St Ann Street premises which eventually linked up the two previously separate museums. These extensions meant that recent discoveries from important sites such as Old Sarum and Stonehenge were prominently displayed. In 1923 a house and yard to the west of the Museum was purchased and a lecture theatre built by public subscription as a memorial to E T Stevens.

Frank Stevens wanted to develop a more local focus for the museums and reduce the international element of the collections. Egyptian artefacts were transferred to the Bournemouth Natural Science Society in the 1920s. After Dr Humphrey Blackmore's death he began to dispose of items from the Blackmore Museum, starting with the Squier and Davis collection which was sold to the British Museum. This process of disposal continued, so by the 1950s there was little left of the original Blackmore Museum collection and the building became effectively an annex to Salisbury Museum. The Blackmore Museum title was dropped from the official title of the Museum in 1951.

Despite this rationalisation the collections remained eclectic. Frank Stevens acquired a large number of 'English Domestic By-Gones' from Mr and Mrs Roland Mole of Lymington in 1931. Assembled over a period of 30 years from across the country, the objects ranged from cottage furnishings to roasting equipment and man traps. Like previous curators Frank Stevens was a collector of ceramics and continued to enlarge both his own collection and that of the Museum. Since the museums were controlled by one family, and in the case of Frank Stevens he lived in the St Ann Street premises, the dividing line between what was personal and what was for the museums must have been difficult to maintain.

Frank's wife, Mrs Jean Stevens, also had a major role to play in the development of the Salisbury Museum. She introduced innovative techniques to display the costume collection in the 1930s, used her excellent design skills to produce posters to advertise museum lectures, delivered gallery talks and outside lectures, and held the post of honorary Assistant Treasurer.

Grand Designs

When Frank Stevens died in 1949 Hugh Shortt became the new Curator of the Museum. Under Hugh's leadership the Museum initiated its own archaeological excavations with the formation of the Salisbury Museum Excavation sub-Committee in the 1950s. This voluntary group was later called the Salisbury Museum Archaeological Research Group (SMARG). The group excavated many key sites in the local area including Old Sarum, Gomeldon Medieval village, Laverstock pottery kilns and the City itself.

Plans were developed to find a new home for the Museum in the 1960s. Over 100 years of collecting and the gradual expansion of the St Ann Street premises had created a building that was costly to maintain and impractical as a modern museum. There was also a problem with the museum's location. St Ann Street, once a major route into Salisbury, became a back street with the construction of the ring road. In 1965 the New Sarum Society was formed to raise funds to build, equip and endow a new museum. The Town Mill site was selected as a suitable location, and after an initial period working with architect Sir Basil Spence the Society commissioned Powell and Moya to produce some radical new designs for a Salisbury and Stonehenge Museum.

Unfortunately the scheme for the Town Mill site was to prove too expensive, however there was still an urgent need to find a new home. The final catalyst for a move came in 1975 with the gift of the Pitt Rivers collection, acquired by the remarkable campaign waged by the then chairman, Lord Congleton, and by Peter Saunders, who succeeded Hugh Shortt as Curator in 1975. A separate museum in its own right, the acquisition of the Pitt Rivers collection made finding a new home an absolute necessity.

The King's House became available in 1978 with the closure of the College of Sarum St Michael in the Cathedral Close. The relocation of the Museum was an ambitious move involving a major campaign, not only to purchase a 125 year lease on the King's House from the Dean and Chapter, but also to refurbish the building for the displays and collections. Fundraising events included a three day Sale and Auction of Treasures at the King's House; a Larmer Tree Two day Extravaganza and a Gigantic Plant Sale.

The Giant arrives at his new home in the King's House

The King's House

The 1980s were a period of growth for the Museum. New galleries were opened telling the History of Salisbury and Early Man in South Wiltshire. A specific gallery was built to house the Pitt Rivers collection and there were others dedicated to costume and ceramics, including the recently acquired Brixie Jarvis Wedgwood collection. The Museum won eight national awards, including the Museum of the Year Award in 1985 and organised major exhibitions, such as *Cats* in 1991 – 92, which helped to attract a record breaking 48,000 people to the Museum in that year. In June 1998 the Museum was designated for its archaeological collections. Designation carried no financial support but acted as a mark of quality to potential funding bodies.

After almost 20 years, the Stonehenge gallery was long overdue for refurbishment. Following Designation the work, financed by a new fund and a bequest to the Museum, began. Master-minded by the then Assistant Curator of archaeology, Andrew Deathe, this included interactive exhibits and a replica trilithon. The new gallery was opened by Julian Richards in July 2001. (For more details see 'Making a Stonehenge Gallery' by Andrew Deathe in *Sarum Chronicle* issue 1, 2001)

Peter Saunders made some ambitious and significant acquisitions to the Museum during his time as Director. Treasures such as the Monkton Deverill

Torc, the Warminster Jewel and the Amesbury Archer all helped to raise both the importance and the profile of the archaeological collections. Works of art including Turner's *Stonehenge, A Panoramic View of Ashcombe* and *Mrs Ridout and the Coombe Express* have vastly improved the quality and depth of the Museum's art collection.

In 2002 the temporary exhibition rooms on the ground floor were renovated, with new flooring, lighting and increased security. This enabled major national exhibits such as 'Making History' from the Society of Antiquaries to be displayed. As *Sarum Chronicle* goes to print plans are well underway for the next major exhibition, on John Constable, in 2011.

As the Museum celebrates its 150th year the opportunity has been taken to look back at its history and think about the future. Under new Director Adrian Green there are plans to refurbish the Museum's archaeology galleries and a successful fundraising campaign has been launched with the membership. Indeed one of the consistent factors behind the success of the Museum over the past 150 years has been the help it has received from local people, particularly its subscribers, members and volunteers. Without their vital support the Museum would not be here to celebrate this major milestone.

References

Willoughby, R W H The Salisbury and South Wiltshire Museum in *WANHM* 57, 307-15

Willoughby, R W H The Blackmore Museum in *WANHM* 57, 316-21

Stevens, Frank, *The Salisbury Museums 1861-1947*, 1948

Book Review

Christian Frost, *Time, Space and Order: The Making of Medieval Salisbury*, Peter Lang, Bern 2009; ISBN: 978-3-03911-943-1

For centuries the myth has circulated of an archer being responsible for the site of Salisbury cathedral when it moved from Old Sarum, the contribution of the wounded deer is somewhat more recent.

Because the whole idea is so obviously preposterous, it is still being used (sometimes indeed by guides dressed in pseudo-medieval costume) as a way of introducing the topic, of generating discussion, and extracting more likely suggestions, to reach the historical facts. Anyone who still has a sneaking sympathy for the archer should be obliged to read this excellent book by Christian Frost. In fact I would go so far as to suggest that every cathedral guide should read it, as, despite a few faults, it provides an excellent thesis on how and why the cathedral and city of Salisbury are arranged the way they are. What you see today is not the result of the wild caprices of its creators but a thoughtful rationalization in structural form of some deeply held religious concepts and beliefs.

Through a series of well-written chapters Frost sets out to analize and explain what existed at Old Sarum and why somewhere else was sought for a new cathedral despite the relative youth of the building already there. He goes on to examine the plan and architectural arrangements of the new and old cathedrals, the Close and the city of New Sarum, comparing what we see here with that which existed elsewhere. He links the architecture with the liturgy – the Sarum Use – that took place within the buildings, and associates both with a symbolism that was designed to give earthly expression to the religious ideas; in short the creation of a Heavenly City and a Holy City which were more than just buildings but expressed deeper beliefs. In particular he describes the processional rites that so dominated thirteenth century Salisbury and which explain much of what you can still see today.

Today we generally view churches and cathedrals as architectural constructions and rank them in accordance with their grandeur. So a cathedral is usually grander than a parish church, the cathedral at x is grander than that at y, and so on. What Frost does very successfully is take us into the medieval mind that saw things very differently. To the clergy at Old Sarum the cathedral there was a machine that was used for praying and worshipping God. Its structure did give praise to God but this was secondary. Processions were a key part of the worship process, and different parts of the building would have played host to different enactments of prayer. Similarly the surrounding area would also have played its part, and have been processed through. It is not hard to imagine how the fighting men of the castle viewed such activities and the enthusiasm with which they supported them and perhaps this as much as anything was the cause of the cathedral relocation to the valley below.

So the cathedral at New Sarum represents the ideal: the unencumbered opportunity to develop the ideal space and structure to facilitate prayer and worship. But also – so Frost suggests – the design of the city of New Sarum was affected in the same way.

Perhaps the best way to illustrate this is to use the modern Way of the Cross worship which processes through the streets and into the cathedral. The passion story has a number of incidents which are described in the Bible – being sentenced to death, the three falls, the meeting with his mother, and the process of crucifixion and dying. In the Way of the Cross, each of these events needs to be acted out in a discreet space, and one space needs to follow logically from another. Hence if a modern planner were developing a city to make it suitable for such a process of worship then there would be various constraints placed upon his planning alternatives. Likewise, the city of New Sarum was conceived to facilitate such processional excursions as part of the liturgy. In short it is more than an economic collection of units that are arranged to maximise efficiency or revenue. Instead they are arranged to facilitate the happenings in the cathedral.

The faults in this book are few, the most annoying being a desire to use long and uncommon words that require the reader to divert to a dictionary before the significance of a sentence can be firmly ascertained. Exegesis, anagogical, paradigmatic, dialectical, macroanthropos – to name but a few.

However, apart from this defect, if that is what it is, this is an excellent book. It provides a serious thesis that attempts to explain why Salisbury and its cathedral are the way they are, and while some may dispute the conclusions that are drawn, there can be no doubt about the book's contribution to a serious debate.

John Elliott

Index to Issues 6 (2006) – 10 (2010)

compiled by Sue Johnson

The letter (a) following a name denotes the author of a paper. Local people, places and principal subjects are indexed as are major references to those elsewhere. Places in the gazetteer of RC Lucas' works are not included. References are to issue number and page(s).

Notes on Contributors

Jennifer Acornley has lived in Coombe Bissett since 1969 and has been interested in the history of the parish for many years. In 1997 she obtained an MA in Local History from Bristol University, and since then has been a volunteer cataloguing the archaeology collection at Salisbury Museum.

Keith Blake worked as an administrator in the London Fire Brigade for more than forty years. Retired, he is now a guide in the chapter house at Salisbury Cathedral and is interested in all aspects of the city's history.

Maureen Davidson, a retired Civil Servant, has been a member of the Girl Guide Association (now known as Girl Guiding UK) as a Brownie, Guide and Leader for over 40 years and is now a member of the Trefoil Guild, a group for retired members. She is particularly interested in the history of Girl Guiding in Wiltshire and has written plays and articles on this subject, including a small booklet to celebrate 100 years of Guiding in 2010.

Richard Deane studied Chinese at Oxford and Leeds universities, worked in the building trade and eventually trained as a stonemason at Salisbury Cathedral. In the mid-1990s he set up his own small stonemasonry business and is now retired. He wrote the text of the primarily photographic book *Salisbury in Detail*, published by Salisbury Civic Society in 2009.

John Elliott is an architectural historian who used to teach at the University of Reading and the University of London: Royal Holloway and Bedford New College. He is now retired and lives near Salisbury.

Adrian Green has worked in museums for 13 years. Before becoming Director of Salisbury Museum in 2007 he managed Bromley Museum Service and prior to that worked at the Museum of London. He has a degree in archaeology from University College London, masters in museum studies from Leicester University, and is an associate member of the Museums Association. He lives in Salisbury with his wife and three children.

Winifred Harwood studied history at the University of Winchester and undertook her doctoral research on the consumption of Winchester College in the 15th and 16th centuries. She is the researcher on the Overland Trade project, which uses the Southampton brokage books to illuminate the trade between Southampton and its hinterland 1430-1540.

Sue Johnson is a local historian with a special interest in early Victorian Salisbury.

Kay Taylor gained her PhD from the University of the West of England in 2006 for her thesis on the development of Quakerism in 17th century Wiltshire. She lives near Chippenham and is currently researching the history of Maud Heath's Causeway on behalf of the trustees and is also involved in other local history projects in the area.